To Alida — with fond memories
of all my wonderful years
at the Women's Institute. Th ks
for arranging H
event.

SHAKESPEARE'S COMEDIES OF PLAY

SHAKESPEARE'S COMEDIES OF PLAY

J. Dennis Huston

Columbia University Press
New York   1981

Copyright © 1981 J. Dennis Huston

Printed in Hong Kong

Library of Congress Cataloging in Publication Data

Huston, J   Dennis.
  Shakespeare's comedies of play.

  Includes bibliographical references and index.
  1.   Shakespeare, William, 1564–1616 – Comedies.
I.   Title.
PR2981.H85   1981   822.3′3   80–21366
ISBN 0–231–05142–5

For Priscilla Jane, Kate, and Penn
who would rather have had my time

Contents

Acknowledgments

First books, particularly first books which do not appear at the onset of one's academic career, have deep and long-standing debts to clear. It is my pleasure, at last, to set about this business, though I am also fully aware that the nature of my subject carries with it immeasurable obligations to past scholars: our greatest debts, after all, are the ones we no longer recognize as debts. As best I could, however, I have identified ideas borrowed from others in my footnotes. Here I want to record more general – and less easily footnoted – kinds of indebtedness.

As a student I was encouraged at crucial times by three teachers, Edward T. Hall, John Maguire and Alvin Kernan, who thus changed the direction of my life and helped me to think of myself as one who might some day similarly affect some of my students. Because Al Kernan in addition directed my dissertation and then years later read the manuscript of this study, offering encouragement and suggestions for revision, my debt to him is most obvious and extensive.

As a teacher I have been regularly taught and encouraged by my students, who first pointed me in the direction of this study and then showed continuing interest both in the project itself and in the ideas included in it. There were times, in fact, when their excitement about these ideas was the clearest proof I had that the ideas made sense.

My colleagues and friends at Rice University have also offered generous portions of their time, interest, advice, and emotional support. Many of the ideas in this work grew indirectly out of the experience of acting in Shakespeare productions with Wes Morris, Terry Doody and John Bouchard – as we all tried, in rehearsal and discussion, to figure out just what Shakespeare was doing in these often perplexing plays. At different times Jane Nitzsche and Alan Grob read this manuscript and offered the same helpful suggestion for improving it, and I could have saved myself a good deal of work and some considerable disappointment if I had not stubbornly resisted their suggestion for almost two years. Of all my colleagues, though, I am most deeply indebted to David Minter, who not only read the manuscript – some portions in several drafts – and offered useful advice but also, as my playing partner in a countless number and variety of games, has helped me to understand that we do not have to give up play just because we have to give up youth.

At various stages in its growth this study was read by scholars who offered me help of one sort or another. Sylvan Barnet, James Calderwood, Sherman Hawkins and David Young, in the midst of busy schedules, found time and kind words for the work of a writer they had never even met. And Robert Egan read this manuscript with the care and consideration that all writers hope will be afforded their work. His enormously detailed and thoughtful suggestions eventually enabled me to shape this study into its final, publishable form.

While working on this book, I had the help of three different typists, Audrey Handley, Sue Davis and Erma Turner, who patiently made their way through an almost unending series of foul papers. And during this time Rice University provided generous financial support, not only by assisting with typing and later with publication expenses, but also by providing me with a semester of sabbatical leave in which to write without interruption.

Parts of the chapters on *A Midsummer Night's Dream* and *The Taming of the Shrew* appeared originally in *SEL* and in *Shakespeare Studies*, and I am grateful to the editors of these journals for permission to reprint this material here.

Finally, I want to acknowledge support so freely and lovingly given that I continually took it for granted: from my wife, Priscilla Jane, who listened tirelessly as I first tried to thrash out my ideas, who read even the roughest drafts of this study and gently pulled me back toward sense when I had ridden my hobby-horse beyond the pale of reason, and who continued to have faith in this project even when mine wavered.

Snowmass, Colo.   J. D. H.
August 1980

Introduction: The Comedies of Play

Old myths, particularly old critical myths, die hard. And Shakespeare, as was his wont, promulgated more than his share of myths, both in his plays and in his person. One of them we are all familiar with, partly because it was given the ring of authority by the greatest of English myth-making poets: Shakespeare was a natural genius, essentially untutored and unlearned, who achieved literary greatness simply by warbling his native woodnotes wild. That idea took centuries to die, in spite of massive evidence to the contrary about Shakespeare's learning and about his professional involvement in the theater, as actor, writer, and part-owner. Another myth, almost as old and even more enduring, is that there was a recognizable and tidy pattern to Shakespeare's development as an artist. He began, so this argument goes, by serving a sort of dramatic apprenticeship, during which time he wrote basically unsophisticated (though often commercially successful) plays in which he developed his dramatic and poetic skills. These eventually reached fruition in a great outpouring of dramatic energy that produced his mature, 'great' plays. And then, after this period of productivity, there was a tailing off of dramatic energies that resulted in the strange, sometimes de-energized, and often disjointed plays of the later period.

To both of these myths there is undoubtedly some measure of truth. Shakespeare was not a scholar-writer, like John Milton or Ben Jonson. And he produced most of his greatest plays in the middle of his career. But such ideas also severely limit our understanding of Shakespeare. The first prevents us from seeing the learning and professional skill that provide the underpinnings of Shakespeare's art; the second blinds us to the particular strengths of the early and late works by measuring them against the achievement of the middle plays. Only recently, for instance,

1

have critics, guided by Northrop Frye's re-evaluation of the romances,[1] begun to argue that Shakespeare's later plays are only different from, not necessarily inferior to, the mature works.[2] I think the same thing can be said for some of the early plays, particularly some of the comedies, which have too often been judged deficient because they have been measured against works like *As You Like It*, works richer in characterization, more sophisticated in language, and more complex in world view. For such virtues, though they are highly valued by modern critics, are not the only ones we might value in a play. If, for example, we decided that coherent dramatic action – not an insignificant artistic virtue –were of crucial importance in drama, then almost any early comedy would seem superior to *As You Like It*, which interrupts its main storyline to dally for two acts in the Forest of Arden. Of course, critics do not demand coherent action from *As You Like It*, because it has other, very considerable strengths. So neither, I think, should these critics necessarily demand the virtues of *As You Like It* from earlier works.

The argument of this study, then, is a simple one: we have too long undervalued Shakespeare's early comedies because we have not paid sufficient attention to their particular strengths – to their creative energy, their exuberant experimentation with dramatic convention and, ultimately, their joy in the theatrical medium and in the act of play-making itself. Instead we have been too much concerned with finding in them an outline for the future, marking in their structures, themes and characterizations early strains of a more complex species of comedy to follow, rather than noting the essential characteristics of the species before us. One such characteristic, which I take to be the defining quality of these early comedies, is their playfulness. In them Shakespeare dramatically announces his sense of the way play, in its almost infinite variety, can affect and transform the world; that is, he celebrates his delight in his own creative powers, in the possibilities of drama itself, and in the vital worlds created by the union of such powers with such possibilities. In their celebration of the playwright's near-magical control of his form and medium – and so implicitly of the world itself – these comedies of play give evidence, no less metaphysically serious for being exuberant, that Shakespeare began his career as we now realize he ended it: by dramatizing the artist's urge to play with his world, to order 'reality' as he orders the world of his art.[3] Let us see how.

On the day that he himself has appointed for his marriage to Kate in *The Taming of the Shrew*, Petruchio does not arrive as expected for the wedding, and as the family and friends of Baptista Minola wait uneasily for an arrival they fear may never come, they offer various explanations for the groom's delay: Petruchio means to shame them; he is mad and therefore not to be trusted; he is a man of his word and has been somehow unavoidably delayed by fortune. Each of the speakers, it is clear, is acquainted with a Petruchio different from the one known to the others. To Baptista, he is a proud young lord from Verona whose irresistible self-assurance may now signal villainy; to Kate, he is a madman who may now be making a joke of her feelings, as he earlier made a joke of reality itself; while to Tranio, he is one who, because he has earlier made good his word against impossible odds, must now be trusted, even though his present absence is inexplicable. What such discrepant opinions of Petruchio here suggest, besides the uncertainty of Kate's wedding, is the very uncertainty of human personality itself. Like Petruchio, man is a player of roles who appears in different guises before different people. In a sense, he is an actor on the stage of life fleshing out a variety of roles to which he gives his own very personal sort of interpretations. And if unlike the actor, man does not find his parts already composed or his world tidily coherent, he at least tries to bring to his roles the ordering effects of composition and coherence: he would play his parts with the convincing style of a well-practised actor and he would find or impose coherence on the unpredictable welter of his life.

All this is no doubt a commonplace observation; it was not new when Petronius gave voice to it two thousand years ago: *totus mundus agit histrionem* – all the world plays the actor. And it still commands attention today, as the recent studies of sociological theorists like Erving Goffman and Elizabeth Burns[4] have made clear. What is not commonplace about this observation, though, is the use to which it was put by Shakespeare, who returned obsessively in his plays to what Anne Righter in her brilliant book of that title[5] calls the 'idea of the play', to that moment when, as Sidney Homan argues,[6] 'the theater turns to itself' – when the dramatist turns away from the images regularly employed in other art forms and focuses instead on the uniqueness of his own medium, on the theater itself. In such a moment man appears as an actor playing out his life before other actors and an audience of distant spectators he never sees. And in such a moment too Shakespeare not only turns the theater to itself, but turns his audience that way as well. Those spectators who are suddenly made conscious that they watch people who are only actors may necessarily wonder if they also are people who, from another perspective, appear merely as actors. Moreover, this use of the theatrical metaphor may turn the members of the audience to themselves in another way: they may become conscious that Shakespeare is playing with their emotions and thoughts, manipulating them, in some of the same ways that he is manipulating his characters. For a time at least the audience may, like the characters, be under the control of the playwright. Granted that control is not as extensive as the playwright wields over his characters – an audience can at any moment turn away from a play as a character cannot – but it is control nevertheless, and so strengthens the metaphorical association between audience and character, between man and actor. Temporarily the boundary between the stage and life dissolves as the play reaches out to touch the audience partly by reminding it of its *role* as audience.

It is perfectly possible, for example, that members of an audience watching a production of *The Taming of the Shrew*, and waiting for Petruchio to arrive for his wedding, might become conscious during the interlude I have just described that they are themselves watching an audience waiting for Petruchio to arrive for his wedding. For like the people who have come to Kate's wedding, Shakespeare's audience has gathered in a ceremonious way upon a special occasion to observe a kind of ritualized spectacle, complete with costumes and a foreordained script. In different ways each group has entered into the realm of play, as Johan Huizinga defines the term:

> play is a voluntary activity or occupation executed within certain fixed limits of time and place, according to rules freely accepted but absolutely binding, having its aim in itself and accompanied by a feeling of tension, joy and the consciousness that it is 'different' from 'ordinary life.'[7]

A wedding is not, of course, to be exactly equated with a stage comedy, but both are similar in being festive occasions set apart in time and space from the world of ordinary events and activities. In this instance, too, the similarities between a play and a wedding are reinforced by complementary correspondences, since the stage comedy is about to present its audience with a wedding that is in fact a kind of stage comedy. In addition both the wedding party and the play's audience, though for different reasons, impatiently await Petruchio's arrival so that the festivities can begin. At the beginning of this scene, then, Shakespeare plays with two audiences as he prepares them for Petruchio's re-entry. In the process he intensifies dramatic tension and at the same time turns the audience watching his play in upon itself; he both plays with its responses and calls attention to the fact that he is playing with its responses. Why he does so the subsequent entrance of Biondello makes clear.

As we and the wedding party await Petruchio's arrival, Biondello brings news of him and of his imminent entry. That news is presented in such a way, though, as to bring a temporary halt to the action of the play. For a moment the forward momentum of plot is forgotten, as Shakespeare focuses the attention of both his audiences on Biondello's performance. Bearing the news everyone wants to hear, Biondello first tantalizes his audience by quibbling about the difference between the phrases 'is coming' and 'is come,' next delivers a bravura description of Petruchio's dress, groom and horse, and finally dances off in self-satisfied delight. For this brief moment a minor character hardly noticeable in the rest of the play (where he never has a speech longer than six lines and usually speaks only one or two lines at a time) commands stage center.

Such a dramatic interlude can be accounted for in any number of ways. It gives evidence of Shakespeare's capacity to provide actors with God's plenty by bringing even minor parts to sudden moments of life; it prepares both Shakespeare's audience and Petruchio's for the outlandishness of his behavior during the wedding scene; it provides this play, rich throughout in opportunities for performance, with yet another spectacular dramatic set-piece; and it suggests the way in which Petruchio's energetic capacity for playing roles magically inspires and touches off performances in those he makes contact with – not only by Biondello here but also by Gremio immediately after the wedding, by Grumio after the wedding journey and, most importantly, by Kate first on the road back to Padua and then at her sister's wedding celebration. Of these explanations the last is of most particular interest to me here, because it points the way of this study – to Shakespeare's abiding concern in his early comedies not only with 'the idea of the play' but also with the idea of play itself.

Like the statement that all men play the actor, to which it is closely linked, this observation is a kind of commonplace. Players of one type or another are everywhere in Shakespeare, not only among his clowns and fools (Feste, Touchstone, and Bottom) and comic heroes and heroines (Petruchio, Berowne, and Rosalind) but also among his villains (Richard III, Iago, and Edmund) and tragic heroes (Richard II and Hamlet). Moreover, criticism in recent years, turning away from the New Critics' concern with plays as essentially dramatic poems,[8] has directed an ever-increasing amount of attention to qualities and characteristics of play and play-making in Shakespearean drama.[9] It is hardly surprising, then, that the works examined in this study show Shakespeare playing with the contingencies of plot, staging an almost endless series of plays-within-plays, manipulating conventions and expectations in order to play with his audiences' responses, engaging his characters in games of elaborate wordplay, offering events and characters out of the play worlds of fairy-tale and make-believe, delighting almost like a child in the play of his own newly discovered powers, playing with the difficulties and challenges of playwriting by drawing attention to them, and presenting characters who play out consciously elaborate dramatic performances before their own audiences as well as Shakespeare's. In play, such evidence suggests, Shakespeare found – at least while he was writing the early comedies – nothing less than an existential address to the world. For him, as for Schiller, man may have seemed 'only fully a human being when he plays.'[10] Let us see why.

Play, and most particularly child's play, is an attempt to mediate between the self and the outside world by an exercise of control. For a time the child in his little world, or microsphere,[11] and the adult in the carefully delimited realms of his games manages the inchoate welter of reality by subjecting it to forms and schemes he has constructed. Temporarily he manipulates reality by bringing it under the control of his very particular purposes, though this control must necessarily be both temporary and in part illusory. 'To hallucinate ego mastery,' Erik Erikson writes, 'and yet also to practice it in an intermediate reality between phantasy and actuality is the purpose of play . . .'[12] Such a definition of play, though, relates it to activities which we normally think of as different from play, namely working and learning. For in order to work at or learn something we must first be able to subject it to managing forms and schemes already known; we must bring it in some way under the control of the ego. Work, learning, and play then may not be as different as we usually suppose. After all, work and learning, almost as much as play, may be, in Huizinga's words quoted earlier, 'a voluntary activity or occupation executed within certain fixed limits of time and place, according to rules freely accepted but absolutely binding . . .' For this reason Jean Piaget, perhaps the foremost modern theorist of the meaning and nature of child's play, argues[13] that play is merely one of the aspects, or poles, of almost any activity.

The real difficulty in our attempt to find a satisfactory definition of play, Piaget claims, 'lies perhaps in the fact that there has been a tendency to consider play as an isolated function . . . and therefore to seek particular solutions to the problem, whereas play is in reality one of the aspects of any activity'.[14] What defines play for Piaget then is the ever-present but ever-changing nature of the relationship between the self and reality. When in this relationship reality predominates, the result, according to Piaget, is accommodation, the adjustment of the organism to imposing demands from without; when the self predominates, the result is assimilation, the absorption of reality to the demands of the organism. The first sort of predominance, Piaget argues, produces imitation; the second, play. And when something like a balance is struck between accommodation and assimilation the result is 'serious' thought: 'If every act of intelligence is an equilibrium between assimilation and accommodation, while imitation is a continuation of accommodation for its own sake, it may be said conversely that play is essentially assimilation, or the primacy of assimilation over accommodation.'[15]

The attractiveness of Piaget's explanation of play is apparent to anyone who has ever found in his own work the joy and fun ordinarily associated with child's play: play is to be defined not by what one does but by how one does it. It is not some isolated function or activity to be juxtaposed to work but rather a state of mind, an address to the world. To the extent that the self can master, control, assimilate the world around it, it attains to play: and although there can be in Piaget's system almost no such thing as perfectly pure play, since any act of assimilation must also involve some measure of accommodation, there is conversely no activity which cannot become play. Before Piaget, theorists of play have opposed it to work, even when that work seemed obviously related to play – as in professional sports, where paid participants earn money while they 'play'. But if we think of play as essentially an address to the world by which the self proclaims its mastery of reality, we can account for the fact that professional sports, like any other activity, *can* be play. For instance, in his first years with the Giants, Willie Mays played baseball in the Polo Grounds with the same spontaneous joy and energy that compelled him when the game was over to join in children's games of stickball on the streets outside the stadium. For him professional baseball was play, and as if to signal this fact, Mays developed a distinctive way of catching fly balls, in 'basket catches' that dramatically enacted, perhaps by intuition, what Piaget calls assimilation. Instead of receiving flies in the traditional self-protective way of accommodation, in front of his face, Mays allowed them to drop into his lap, or belly, almost as if he were swallowing – assimilating – them. Baseball, Mays so announced, was child's play for him.

And what Willie Mays made out of baseball Shakespeare may have made out of playwriting, at least near the beginning of his career. I do not mean to imply by this statement that Shakespeare, warbling his native woodnotes wild without a real thought for what he was doing, found himself suddenly a star in the major leagues of the London theater world. I mean rather that in his occupation with the theater, both as an actor and writer of plays, Shakespeare may have discovered and celebrated the power of play as a supremely human achievement. Within the compass of the theater, manipulating the reality of actors, stage, and audience around him so that they became temporarily a world as he himself defined it, Shakespeare may have found himself playing not only with the theater but with life itself. In the continuing confrontation between self and world, he may, like a child at play, have temporarily felt himself assimilating and becoming that world he confronted. For in a way a stage offers a playwright a grown-up version of a child's play-world – a literalized microsphere, circumscribed in time and space, where the imagination assimilates, manipulates, and reshapes – masters – reality. And such mastery was emphasized in the Elizabethan theater not only by the presence of an audience to applaud the playwright's powers and share his vision, but also by the conscious correlation of theater, with its heavens above and pit below, to world. To this insulated world, implicitly an image of reality mastered by the playwright, Shakespeare in his early comedies brought an exuberant delight in the exercise of his powers, both as a dramatist and as an assimilator of reality.

The first four plays in this study, for example, are all dramatically different from one another, as if Shakespeare were trying out different principles of organization in each work – focusing on plot in *The Comedy of Errors*, on language in *Love's Labour's Lost*, on the player-hero in *The Taming of the Shrew*, and reflexively on the act of writing a successful play in *A Midsummer Night's Dream*. In these four plays, too, the playwright who so successfully and self-consciously manipulates the theatrical medium to his purposes, assumes a prominent role in the action – sometimes making his presence known through surrogate figures like Berowne, Petruchio, and Oberon, sometimes calling attention to himself as the manipulator of plot and action by the very *way* he manipulates plot and action. This he does most obviously in *The Comedy of Errors*, where he plays almost exclusively with the dramatic possibilities of plot, moving two sets of identical twins through a series of mistakings and mistimings that depend for their success upon elaborate authorial manipulation. The extent of this manipulation he emphasizes – and makes fun of – not only by matching each set of identical twins with identical names but also by emphasizing the discrepancies between what the audience and the characters know of the circumstances. From a position of detached amusement, the audience observes the characters, as they construct one logical but faulty explanation after another, trying, but failing, to assimilate the monster of reality which confronts them. Meanwhile, secure in its knowledge of the dramatic situation, the audience sees as play what the characters experience as madness.

In *Love's Labour's Lost* Shakespeare turns away from his earlier concern with plot and instead concentrates on language and the uses to which man puts it as he constructs schemes and pageants to suit reality to his desires. And although no one in this work altogether succeeds in finding a language to control either self or world, Shakespeare plays with the characters' failures and converts them to his success. He assimilates their interrupted schemes and pageants into his own interrupted, but coherent, pageant. *The Taming of the Shrew* and *A Midsummer Night's Dream*, at the thematic center of this study, present play, as process and product, attaining almost to transcendence. In their celebration of, and play with, the possibilities of the theatrical medium itself, these works have perhaps never been surpassed: to the creator of the Padua which Petruchio conquers and the Athens which Theseus governs almost anything seems possible, and proves so.

In *The Taming of the Shrew* an Induction of enormous dramatic energy that plays through a series of Pirandello-like variations upon the theme of illusion and reality demonstrates the ambivalence of its ties to both reality and illusion by proving simultaneously illusory – it is soon abandoned without apparently having to do with Shakespeare's play of shrew-taming – and real – it *is* retained as an Induction to that play and does dramatically prepare an audience to understand Petruchio's methods and purposes in his dealings with Kate. Then, too, Petruchio himself proves to be Shakespeare's most obviously successful player. Unlike Richard III, who collapses after he acts his way to success, and Rosalind, who must at last depend heavily upon the miracle-working powers of the playwright *ex machina*, Petruchio succeeds on his own in making reality over in the image of his desires. As actor, director, gamesman, and wordplayer who magically metamorphoses and masters the world that is all before him, Petruchio offers us the image of the player and playwright as all-conquering hero. In *A Midsummer Night's Dream* we feel the powers of the playwright not so much in his hero as in the achievement of the play itself – in the way Shakespeare interrelates separate and apparently disparate plots, juggles the mistakings of Puck and the lovers in the woods, plays tricks with both historical and dramatic time, converts metaphor to dramatic action and dramatic action to metaphor, and finally, makes of the mechanicals' failed play his own supremely comic success. In the process he suggests, and at once dramatically demonstrates, how the playwright may achieve and express a 'most rare vision' at once transcending the limitations of his form and parodying his own success as a dramatist.

This vision, however, undergoes modification in the later

comedies, where the exuberant optimism of a playwright celebrating the near-magical union of creative power with dramatic possibility gives way to a more qualified, mature view of the powers available to the play-maker, both within the world of the theater and within the theater of the world. In place of striking theatrical pyrotechnics, these mature plays offer us other virtues – characters of fuller form and feeling, a wider range of emotional experience, and dramatic worlds of greater complexity. In these worlds characters must confront – and attempt to assimilate – a reality which threatens them not only with accident, misunderstanding, and confusion, but also with evil acting through malevolent human agents.

To be sure, such a problem once appears as a passing concern in *The Two Gentlemen of Verona*, the only early comedy omitted from this study – because it lacks the creative energy and exuberant playfulness of these other works.[16] In that play Shakespeare first brings into his comic world the problem of evil intention, long before it appears with regularity in *The Merchant of Venice*, *Much Ado About Nothing*, *As You Like It*, and *Twelfth Night*. For this reason *The Two Gentlemen of Verona* serves as the exception which proves the rule in the early comedies. Also, its evil character does not really resemble Shylock, Don John, Duke Frederick, or Malvolio, for Proteus begins as one of the heroes and comes to villainy only after he has fallen in love with Silvia. Because we first think of Proteus as a hero, his straying into evil-doing seems more a temporary derangement than a habit of mind, as it is with the later villains. Thus evil in *The Two Gentlemen of Verona* seems a passing aberration, not something present from the first, apparently in the very order of things. The presence of evil in the later comedies does not, however, signal the disappearance of play from these works. In them the dramatist still calls himself to our attention by reminders that the play before us is a play; and characters still, like Petruchio, stage-manage scenes and act out parts, directing others toward comic resolutions. Then too, at least once in these later works, in the Forest of Arden, play proceeds at length with the energy and assumes the magical, transforming powers that it enjoys in the earlier works. But in general its powers are qualified. The Forest of Arden is a realm clearly separated from a containing world of arbitrary, intrusive violence; and before Rosalind, Orlando, and Duke Senior can make their way to the wish-fulfilling theater of the forest, they must first take flight from a dark world of tyranny, which would stifle not only the impulses of play but also the very energies of life itself. Much the same thing is true also of *The Merchant of Venice*. In this work Portia assumes a disguise, travels from Belmont to Venice, and then plays with the language of law first to emphasize Shylock's literalism and then to turn that literalism against him. Of the courtroom she makes a stage, where she directs and acts in a spectacularly successful play of her own composition. But before she succeeds, Shylock, intent on murder, raises his knife over Antonio's heart. And Shylock is not, like Duke Frederick, a cardboard villain. So convincing, in fact, are his hatred and his capacity to commit murder, as well as his feelings of persecution, that he becomes a focus of dramatic attention too powerful to be forgotten, even in defeat. The success of Portia's play never entirely dispels either the threat of evil or the dramatic force embodied in Shylock. In *Twelfth Night*, too, play has only a limited sphere of success. Surrounding the insulated kingdom of Illyria there is another world, of darker designs and experiences, which includes the sea of lost identity, of shipwrecks and drownings, of violent battles and purposes mistaken. This world also includes, as Feste's closing lyric makes clear, endings which may not abide 'happily ever after,' for that song ends the play by reminding us that precipitous marriages like the ones performed and promised in this work produce happy resolutions only in the world of comic convention. In life, marriages entered into in delusion quickly come to grief in the face of wind and rain.

Perhaps the clearest demonstration of the differences in tone between the early and the later comedies, however, is provided by the particulars of *Much Ado About Nothing*, and for that reason I have included it as the conclusion to this study, not necessarily because I think it the most representative of the later plays – though it is surely representative in a way that a work like *The Merry Wives of Windsor*, or even *The Merchant of Venice*, is not – but because its obvious likenesses to the earlier comedies make its differences all the more striking. Consider, for instance, its similarities to *The Taming of the Shrew*.

In both plays young men in a holiday mood arrive in a world where an old man watches over his two daughters (or a daughter and a niece), one of whom is quiet, well-behaved, and passive;

the other, sharp-tongued, quick-witted, and enormously energetic. Also for each of these young women there is a dramatically appropriate young man: one conventionally minded and proper in his behavior; the other, more outspoken and brasher in his carriage. In both works the less conventionally minded lovers are brought together by the design of the young man's friends, and in each case there is an extended verbal battle rife with sexual suggestiveness before the woman, still protesting, succumbs to the man's advances. Both plays, too, contain near their centers a wedding scene in which the regular order of things is shattered by the unexpected behavior of the groom. In the process much ado is made about the question of dress and with it, of seemingly misjudged character until apparent violence is done to the bride, and the groom makes a self-consciously dramatic exit. Finally, in both plays the possibly disastrous consequences of the disordered weddings are mitigated by subsequent events, which ultimately bring the groom back to the scene of the wedding, unveil as a new bride the old one restored to her imagined perfection, and unite both sets of lovers in a double marriage celebration which closes the play. The remarkable number of similarities between these two comedies suggests that either consciously or unconsciously Shakespeare had the outlines of *The Taming of the Shrew* in mind while writing *Much Ado About Nothing*. The later play may be a revision, in both senses of the word, of the former. Just what the nature of that revision is, and how it reflects Shakespeare's changing view of the powers inherent in play, it is now the purpose of this study to show.

1 Playing with Discontinuity: Mistakings and Mistimings in *The Comedy of Errors*

The Comedy of Errors announces Shakespeare's joy in play-making to the world, for it is the work of a dramatist who, above all things else, delights in his medium. In it he finds a reality easily assimilated and manipulated by his newly discovered dramatic powers, since he manages the dramatic microcosm with absolute control. He builds a plot of mistaking, self-consciously contrived, and then he exuberantly pushes his characters around the world he has trapped them in, all the while encouraging his audience, which knows the reason for the mistaking, to laugh with him at the characters' vain efforts to understand their situation. By thus drawing attention to his obvious manipulation of plot and medium, Shakespeare keeps his play – in both meanings of the word – between the characters and the audience. As a result, there is no need for any real development of character in *The Comedy of Errors*, since the action derives less from what the characters do than from what the playwright does to them. At times Shakespeare does not even differentiate between characters: the two Dromios really *are* interchangeable. He never allows his characters any substantial complexity: Antipholus of Syracuse seems at first interesting, but he soon becomes as stubbornly one-dimensional as all the other characters in *The Comedy of Errors*. He must, if the play is to succeed, because the complications of its plot depend on the characters' persistent refusal to change either their minds or their behavior. In a sense, then, even the characters serve as props in this play; the playwright gives them, like puppets, a few defining and unchanging features – some of them interchangeable – and then

14

he moves his characters mechanically about as he wills. The action, like that of a puppet show, depends in large measure on physical movement – on 'chance' meetings, misplaced props, and violent altercations. No doubt it is an oversimplification to say that Shakespeare here gives us drama as puppet show. But such an observation does direct us towards the *spirit* of the work, towards its basic dramatic simplicity and its exuberant physical energy. It also makes clearer the correspondence between Shakespeare's play-making here and the world of child's play. Like the child playing, Shakespeare working, and playing, with the 'microsphere' of the theater wields absolute control over a newly manageable object world, not of toys but of actors, costume, and props, which he turns to his particular dramatic uses.

There is, however, at least one notable difference, other than those of intellect and power, between Shakespeare's play and that of the child. The dramatist proffers his play to an audience for approval, while child's play is often, though not always, self-sufficient. And in so addressing an audience, Shakespeare is, at least in part, attempting to extend the range of his mastery; he is including the audience, as well as players, stage, and props, in the world he controls. It is no wonder, then, that Shakespeare's characteristic response to the members of his audience, repeated in an almost endless number of ways in these comedies, is to manipulate them. He manipulates his characters too, and the relationships between these two kinds of manipulation variously define the world of Shakespeare's comedies of play.

In *The Comedy of Errors*, for example, Shakespeare keeps his audience almost always at a distance from the action. As its title implies, the work is nearly unmitigated farce. For with its dependence on mistaken identity, mistiming, rapid movement, slapstick violence, exaggerated reactions, and outrageous puns, this play has almost as much in common with a Marx brothers movie as with other Shakespearean comedies. It is also, in some obvious ways, Shakespeare's most simply conceived dramatic work, since all of the action develops out of a single basic misunderstanding, a fact known from the beginning to the audience but withheld from all the characters until the end.[1] As a result, the audience watches the play from a position of almost godlike superiority; it shares with the playwright the secret that very simply explains all the confusion.

The characters, of course, have no such knowledge. They do not know they are characters in a farce; nor are they granted the divine overview offered to the audience, so they continually try to make logical sense out of the confused welter, the discontinuity, of their experiences. They construct hypotheses to account for others' strange, inconsistent behavior, blaming it on jest, drunkenness, madness, witchcraft, adultery, breach of contract, or thievery. And although these hypothetical explanations are erroneous, they are all more logical and probable, more sensible, than the answer ultimately revealed to these characters. For that answer is purposely ridiculous, the playful invention of a dramatist calling attention to his own imaginative energies as he makes dramatic sense, and comedy, out of the most wildly improbable comic situation he can devise.

What most obviously draws attention to the presence of the playwright in this work is the crucial way that Shakespeare assimilates, and diverges from, his source, Plautus' *Menaechmi*, where there is only one set of identical twins. By doubling the number of twins – and so geometrically increasing the possibilities for confusion provoked by mistaking – Shakespeare abandons any concern with realism and instead focuses his audience's attention on his capacity to play freely and inventively with the exigencies of a comic plot.[2] In the process he associates his art with play in a number of different forms – as release, by daring to overgo his source's already strained use of unrecognized twins with the same name; as spontaneous invention and fun, by delighting his audience and no doubt himself with ever more ridiculous and exaggerated mistakings; and finally, as the technical skill of playwriting, by manipulating basic dramatic problems of plotting and stage business so that the misunderstandings are continually expanded and intensified, until they threaten the social order of Ephesus with apparent chaos: near the end of the play the bonds of marriage, friendship, service, business contracts, and law, which structure society and give coherent form to life in Ephesus, all apparently dissolve, as husband turns savagely against wife, master against servant, and debtor against creditor.

Nothing people *within* the world of the play can do will resolve the violent disputes. The characters try to bring order out of the chaos that develops during the fifth act, but they meet only with more confusion. When they appeal to the representative of the

Church for help, the Abbess tricks the woman who addresses her, supplies an explanation that immensely oversimplifies the problem at hand, and then retreats with material witnesses into the secluded and detached realm of the priory. Then the Duke, representative of law and social order in Ephesus, proves no more successful than the Church in dealing with the chaos. When both of the principal litigants in the dispute call on him for 'justice,' he listens carefully to strange and conflicting accounts of all that has happened, accounts which are inconsistently corroborated and contradicted by witnesses on both sides of the argument, and then he concludes, helplessly, that 'you are all mated or stark mad' (v. i. 281).[3] They are not. But they *are* manipulated, because as characters in a comic farce they are subject to the arbitrary control of a playwright who moves them about – who plays with them – at his pleasure, and the audience's.

There is, then, an enormous discrepancy between the characters' experience of their dilemma and the audience's experience of the same situation. No doubt there is always a substantial difference between what an audience and the characters experience of a play. However life-like it may be, art is never really life for an audience, and it is never anything else for the characters. But almost always in Shakespearean drama there are effects that work to promote audience engagement in, as well as detachment from, the action.[4] We may be attracted to the wit and energy of a comic hero or heroine, or identify with the struggles and suffering of a tragic hero, or nod in assent at the wisdom in the folly of a clown. And even when a dramatic effect works apparently for detachment, as Shakespeare's use of the play within a play almost always does, its ultimate thematic purpose may be to encourage our intellectual engagement in the dramatic situation. By watching an audience of foolish young lovers ignore the relevance of a play about foolish young lovers in *A Midsummer Night's Dream*, we may realize that we are thereby being encouraged to become a better audience than the one before us. By watching an Induction that is a series of plays within plays in *The Taming of the Shrew*, we may be prepared to see the shrew-taming action which follows as a more complex version of the same sort of imaginative playing.

In *The Comedy of Errors*, however, Shakespeare depends for his principal dramatic effect upon the *dis*engagement of the audience from the characters; the audience is continually encouraged to enjoy its superior knowledge and to laugh at the foolish mistakings of the bewildered characters. Because they know nothing, and the audience knows everything about their predicament, these characters appear laughable in their confusion. In spite of the fact that they are bodied forth on the stage by real people, the characters seem like mechanical imitations of human beings. They entertain us by threatening and inflicting upon one another violence that does not hurt, by posturing emotions that they put aside almost in the next moment, and by moving rapidly about, never settling for long enough in one place to recognize that it is they and not their world which has suddenly started spinning crazily about. The play is, in short, an almost perfect example of Bergson's definition of comedy, of the mechanical imposing itself on the human.

Almost. But not quite – because Shakespearean comedy is never as neat as a general critical summary would have it, never as tidy as its happy endings imply. For there are always in the comedies problems which never get fully resolved. These seem most often to be embodied in the fates of characters who are not included in the final celebrations and who are usually tied, in one way or another, to violence – characters like Malvolio, Don John, and Shylock. But the problems suggested by the figure of the **unreconciled outsider** are not the only ones which regularly cast a shadow across the bright surface of Shakespearean comedy; they are merely the best known. Another, similar kind of difficulty is presented by Shakespeare's use of the misleading beginning, which, though it may not qualify the final festivities, still reminds us from the first of the chaotic forces of disruption and discontinuity which comedy must either reorder or render harmless.

In *The Comedy of Errors* and *A Midsummer Night's Dream*, for example, Shakespeare begins as if his play were going to be a tragedy. Forces of dissolution threaten the world and characters of these plays: Egeon and Hermia, both separated from their families and from an earlier life of joy, face the judgment of a harsh law which menaces them and which not even the ruling Duke can countermand. There are forces of dissolution, too, at the beginning of *The Taming of the Shrew* and *Much Ado About Nothing*, though they threaten the form rather than the content of the play: in both of these works the playwright apparently cannot get his plot smoothly under way. The Induction of *The Taming of the Shrew*, lurching through a sequence of fitful beginnings, is finally altogether abandoned once Shakespeare introduces the story of Kate and Petruchio. And the first act and a half of *Much Ado About Nothing*, spinning out a tangled web of misunderstandings and mistakings, presents a villainous scheme to divide Don Pedro and Claudio, which, apparently following the promise of the play's title, comes at last to absolutely nothing.

The false beginning, as Shakespeare uses it, then, gives a dramatized example of the disorder or discontinuity that the comic dramatist must overcome, both in his play and by his play. If he succeeds in triumphing over this disorder, the proof of the playwright's victory will appear in the comic ending, when resolutions can be worked with miraculous ease. There, what once appeared as chaos proves to be merely part of a larger pattern of order: the storm-tossed sea, which once incomprehensibly divided Egeon's family, just as incomprehensibly brings that family together again. There, what no man before had the power to oppose, is effortlessly put away with a word: 'It shall not need; thy father hath his life' (v. i. 390). Such a reversal is not really, as it first seems, a thematic inconsistency, because the whole play has intervened to make the change possible; the threatening chaos of the beginning is displayed by a comic view of life dramatically realized within the play. And at the same time the play, having attained to the order of art, offers the audience and the playwright proof of a temporary victory over the threatening chaos of life outside the theater.

The best way, though, to understand Shakespeare's complex use of what I have called the misleading beginning is to examine one in detail. *The Comedy of Errors*, by its very title, gives its audience a good idea about what kind of play it is, a knockabout farce built upon mistakings; but the title, however aptly it may be suited to the play as a whole, hardly prepares an audience for the first scene. For there, in an announced 'comedy of errors,' Shakespeare sounds the notes of tragedy – or perhaps of romance,[5] since the pathos of Egeon's tale, with its references to fortune, its interpolated life stories, and its account of a wife and child lost at sea, might suggest the outlines of romance to an experienced Elizabethan playgoer. But whether the beginning suggests tragedy or romance, it must seem confusing and

discontinuous to an audience prepared for a 'comedy of errors.'
Consider, for instance, the opening speech:

> Proceed, Solinus, to procure my fall
> And by the doom of death end woes and all. (I. i. 1–2)

This hardly sounds like a beginning. The end-stopped verses,
with their emphasis on death, doom, end, and fall, and their
heavily accented rhymes, seem much more suited to an exit than
to an entrance; and Egeon undoubtedly means them to be exit
lines, since he is prepared for a judgment of death. At the
beginning of a comedy we confront what appears to be the
ending of a tragedy – an old man speaking his last words before
being led to execution. His words, too, suggest how dominant
the idea of death will be in this first scene, where we hear of
'mortal and intestine jars' (11), of merchants executed, of laws
that promise death to 'any Syracusian born' (19), of an agent's
sudden demise, of the heavens' 'doubtful warrant of immediate
death' (69), of near drowning, of a wife and child lost and feared
dead, and of a second child perhaps lost in search of the first. Here
surely is a scene filled with sorrow and tragedy, a fact emphasized
not only by Egeon's despair at his hopeless condition but also by
repeated references to the arbitrariness of the powers that
persecute him. He is condemned by a law he cannot even have
known about, since the enmity between Syracuse and Ephesus
has sprung up 'of late' (5), and Egeon has not been in Syracuse for
five years. Earlier he has been separated from his wife and child
by a chance accident at sea. And earlier still he has been called
away from the embraces of his wife by his business agent's
apparently sudden death, which has left the care of his goods 'at
random' (43). Egeon seems indeed, as the Duke describes him,
one 'whom the fates have mark'd/To bear the extremity of dire
mishap!' (141–2).

But Egeon's story and the first scene are not really as tragic as
they initially appear, since they may, as I have already suggested,
trace the outlines of romance, with its promise of miraculous
renewal, rather than of tragedy, with its focus on immeasurable
loss. Even more to the point, they *are* part of a play which will
ultimately prove a comedy. And finally, and most significantly,
a number of details *within* the first scene qualify its apparently
tragic tone. The first of these details is the fact that Egeon is not

an altogether reliable narrator. In general what he says about the events of his past life is true, at least as far as we can tell, but he sometimes jumbles the particulars of these events, and his interpretation of their meaning is often misleading. For example, Egeon has a tendency to see only the worst in a situation. He begins the story of his life of 'griefs unspeakable' (33) as if it were one uninterrupted tale of woe. But it is not, for he gives an account of salvation as well as loss, of joy as well as sorrow. Here is the beginning of his story:

> In Syracusa was I born, and wed
> Unto a woman, happy but for me,
> And by me, had not our hap been bad.
> With her I lived in joy; our wealth increased
> By prosperous voyages I often made
> To Epidamnum; till my factor's death
> And the great care of goods at random left
> Drew me from kind embracements of my spouse ... (37–44)

There is in this account a certain discontinuity. Egeon claims that his wife would have been happy but for him and for the fact that their luck was bad, and then he says that they were joyfully married and prosperous. The argument makes no sense. Of course, we know what Egeon means: the sorrow came *after* he and his wife had been happily married for some time, when they were separated. But that is not what Egeon says. So overwhelmed is he by present grief that he makes it color even his account of past joy. In his despair he would reduce the events of his life to the simplistic consistency he sees in them now – to a long series of 'misfortunes' (120) and 'mishaps' (121).

And what Egeon does at the beginning of his story he does throughout: he tries to impose a perfect, uncomplicated continuity on the complex, discontinuous experiences of his life. To some extent, he succeeds in what he attempts, for his story has a convincingly tragic tone and is coherent enough to be easily understood by an audience. In summary that story sounds perfectly continuous and consistent, but in its particulars it is not nearly as neat and tidy as it sounds, for it is rife with inconsistencies both great and small. We have no idea, for instance, how long Egeon and Emilia have been married before they are first separated. By his overriding tone of sadness, Egeon implies that their happiness has been short-lived, a suggestion apparently confirmed by the story of Emilia's pregnancy, which seems the immediate result of the lovers' 'kind embracements' (44). Yet Egeon also explains that after the marriage their wealth increased 'By prosperous voyages I often made/To Epidamnum . . .' (41–42), and this detail suggests a marriage of some substantial length.

There is, of course, good reason for the apparent double time in Egeon's narrative: the marriage *seemed* short because he was so happy and because it is now viewed under the aspect of memory, which sometimes plays tricks with time. In fact, Egeon's memory repeatedly plays such tricks with time during the course of his story; he often shortens or conflates it to give his experience continuity. We do not know, for example, how long he is married before business takes him from his wife, but the time is longer than he implies. Nor do we know how long he and Emilia stay in Epidamnum before setting out for home. More noticeably, we never hear a thing of the years between the separation at sea and the son's eighteenth birthday, a time during which Egeon apparently gave no thought to searching for his lost family. And also, there is a hiatus in his narrative between the time when his son sets out in search of his lost brother and when Egeon undertakes his five-year journey through Greece and Asia, for we later hear that father and son have in fact been separated for seven years (v. i. 309, 320).

In addition, confusion about time is matched in Egeon's story by confusion about details. The twins can be differentiated from one another only by names (53), but they have the same names (129); before the storm Emilia takes care of the latter-born twin (79), but the child who survives with Egeon is 'My youngest boy' (125); when the family faces approaching death at sea, Emilia's tears induce Egeon to seek a means of preservation (75), but it is his wife who initiates the action of fastening herself and the twins to a mast; and finally, the storm that has threatened them all never comes, and the sea at last waxes calm (92), but in this calm sea the ship is 'violently borne upon' a rock (103).

All these inconsistencies undoubtedly can be dismissed as unimportant, as the result merely of Shakespeare's carelessness or inexperience. And, besides, they would never be noticed in a theater, where an audience, responding to Egeon's despair, would interpret his story as he interprets it. But what an audience consciously notices is not always all there is to a play, even for that audience. Drama sometimes reaches below the surface of consciousness to stir the depths beneath, as anyone who has ever watched a good production of *Hamlet* or *King Lear* knows. A play does not, however, have to be a great tragedy to affect an audience more deeply than that audience may consciously know. Even so apparently frothy a work as *The Comedy of Errors* may reach at times beneath the level of an audience's consciousness. It will not go so deep as a great tragedy, but it should not be dismissed as all surface just because it is not *Hamlet* or *King Lear*.

For example, behind the story of Egeon and his separated family in the first scene of *The Comedy of Errors* we may glimpse the outlines of genuinely mythic themes which are everywhere in Shakespearean drama – arbitrary natural violence manifesting itself in storm, confused and uncertain identity,[6] shipwreck on a strange shore, sudden and inexplicable divorce between husband and wife, an old man hopelessly separated from those he loves and wandering in a world of unspeakable griefs, the transforming power of time, the miraculous return of what seems irrevocably lost, and finally, the incomprehensible abundance of great creating nature. More directly to my purposes here, though, is the fact that beneath the surface of this scene we encounter a pattern which will eventually become a dominant thematic concern in the play. That pattern is of the discontinuity of human experience. We have met it first in Shakespeare's confusing beginning, which plays with the audience's expectations about what kind of drama this 'comedy of errors' will be. We have met it next within the realm of the play in Egeon's story, which he tries to make perfectly neat and consistent but which in its small particulars resists his reductively simplifying vision. We can now meet it also in the behavior of the Duke, whose conduct in this scene is inconsistent enough so that even an audience in the theater might take note of it.

Solinus begins by commanding Egeon not to plead his case any longer. But there is nothing in the speech Egeon has delivered which suggests such pleading; the merchant, apparently prepared for a sentence of execution, has called for the Duke to end his woes with the doom of death. For some reason Solinus is not listening to what Egeon is saying, and we soon discover why: he is trying to suppress his sympathy for his prisoner so that he can enforce the harsh law of Ephesus. His first speech is, in fact, a conscious effort to convince himself of the need for Egeon's death. He is not disposed, he claims, – confirming the idea by his denial – to set aside the laws of his country; Syracuse and Ephesus have of late engaged in wars, and the Duke of Syracuse has harshly put Ephesians to death, so Egeon can expect no pity from 'our threatening looks' (10). The sudden shift here from the 'I' of line four to the royal 'we' gives emphasis to the Duke's attempt to act as impersonal justiciary. But he is not as successful at achieving impersonality as he sounds, since he continues to marshal evidence against Egeon, as if he had not yet quite convinced himself to order execution. By the end of the speech, however, the Duke seems to have conquered his impulses for mercy; his conclusion has the ring of inevitability: 'Therefore by law thou art condemn'd to die' (26). Solinus still cannot associate himself with this judgment – the prisoner is condemned 'by law' – but the Duke has at last apparently issued the decree of death. He has no more issued it, however, than he begins to take it away, to delay its enactment: he calls for Egeon to tell his story and to explain what cause drew him to Ephesus. Having begun by ordering his prisoner to plead his case no more, Solinus now in effect commands him to plead it again. The only continuity in the behavior and speeches of this Duke is discontinuity.

And this pattern of apparently discontinuous behavior continues as the scene progresses, for after listening to the first part of Egeon's long account of shipwreck and separation, Solinus encourages him to finish his story, assuring him that 'we may pity, though not pardon thee' (98). The statement is a direct contradiction of the Duke's earlier claim that the outrage perpetrated by the Duke of Syracuse 'Excludes all pity from our threatening looks' (10). Then, when the merchant's tale is finally done, Solinus, moved by the pity which has been implicit in his conduct towards Egeon from the first, delays the execution again. He grants the prisoner a day's reprieve, to allow him time to raise the money necessary for his ransom. Temporarily at least, the Duke puts aside incontrovertible law. His action is thematically significant for at least two reasons. First, it gives evidence that the tragedy threatening both Egeon and this announced 'comedy of errors' can be avoided; it converts the apparent end presented at the beginning of this play to a beginning, and so reinforces a comic pattern established but not recognized in Egeon's story – the pattern of sudden miraculous deliverance from imminent death.

Three times in Egeon's tragic account of his misfortunes he avoids expected ruin: when first he would gladly have accepted his 'doubtful warrant of immediate death' (69), his wife's cries force him to 'seek delays' (75) of their end; when later the sailors, frightened by the approaching storm, have abandoned Egeon and his family on a 'sinking-ripe' (78) ship, the sun unexpectedly disperses the storm clouds (89–90); and when finally this ship is wrecked upon a rock and the family is cast into the sea, they are all soon rescued. Having escaped from it three times in the past, Egeon is now once again delivered from death – by the Duke's reprieve. And though he may view this deliverance, like the ones which preceded it, as fruitless – since his exit lines are as much concerned with death as his first speech was – he is nevertheless exiting to something different from his execution. The tragic pattern initiated by the play's dark beginning has not been dispelled, but it has at least been qualified. The Duke's decision to put off Egeon's execution for a day, then, gives a suggestion of form to traces of comedy obscured by the apparently tragic tone of the first scene. That form will be more fully developed in the scenes that follow.

The second reason why the Duke's reprieve of Egeon's sentence is important is because it makes clearer the relationship between the theme of discontinuity and forms of play in *The Comedy of Errors*. Against the discontinuity of his experience, against the conflict between his human feelings that Egeon should be spared and his sworn duty to enforce an inhuman law, Solinus throws up the defense of a temporary reprieve. For a while he holds the intrusive discontinuity of reality at bay, not, as Egeon has done, by imposing the pattern of tragedy on discontinuous events, but rather by pushing the problem away from him, in time and space: he gives Egeon the rest of the day to search out the money needed to buy release from harsh law, and he turns the prisoner over to the keeping of another. Against law he opposes a temporary reprieve, which creates an insulated world limited in space and time – 'I'll limit thee this day / . . . Try all the friends thou hast in Ephesus' (I. i. 151–3) – to contain Egeon and the problems his story and presence bring to the Duke's consciousness and conscience. But although the Duke partly manipulates this intrusive reality by pushing it away from him, he can find no way to assimilate it effectively, to play with it: as Duke he must enforce the law; as human being he cannot bring himself to do so. Caught between the unyielding rigors of law and the equally compelling dictates of human feeling, he tries to satisfy both demands at once and manages to provide Egeon, and himself, only with a temporary reprieve.

Problems only temporarily pushed aside have a way of returning with redoubled force, however; so when we next see Solinus, in the fifth act, he is besieged on all sides by the apparent discontinuity of reality, which batters at the insulated world of the reprieve. Now all cry for 'justice' (v. i. 133, 190, 194, 197) and demand action from their ruler. In a way this scene presents Solinus with a nightmare version of his earlier experience. Once again he is called upon to render the doom of 'justice'; once again he listens to stories which seek to impose coherence on an apparently discontinuous sequence of events; and once again he finds himself temporarily unable to settle harsh judgment upon those before him. But now he confronts, in place of one difficult decision, many apparently impossible ones; in place of barely discernible discontinuity, an engulfing chaos of contradictions. Where earlier, judgment was rendered difficult because of the discontinuity between the Duke's duty as a ruler and his feelings as a human being, now judgment appears impossible because of raging discontinuity in the very nature of things. Everyone has his own account of events, and none of the accounts matches.

In the conflicting reports of what has happened in Ephesus during the afternoon we find discontinuity in forms we have met before: in the details of the narratives, as with Egeon's tale earlier, and in Solinus' continuing inability to reconcile his duty as a law enforcer with his emotions as a human being:

> She is a virtuous and a reverend lady:
> It cannot be that she hath done thee wrong. (v. i. 134–5)

> Long since thy husband served me in my wars,
> And I to thee engaged a prince's word,
> When thou didst make him master of thy bed,
> To do him all the grace and good I could. (v. i. 161–4)

But in addition we find discontinuity disrupting even the most basic facts of nature, apparently overthrowing the very laws which govern the movement of things in space and time.

Antipholus seems 'borne about invisible' (v. i. 187) or, perhaps more correctly, he seems too *often* visible: here disappearing in retreat behind the walls of the abbey, there appearing in attack after his beating of Dr. Pinch; here dining with his wife and sister-in-law at home, there dining with the courtesan at the Porpentine; here receiving a gold chain of Angelo, there denying that he has ever even seen the chain. In the first scene Egeon's presence threatened the laws of Ephesus; now Antipholus' presence threatens even the laws of nature. Maddening, unassimilable discontinuity, expanding its compass and intensifying its attack, threatens everyone in Ephesus. More than a temporary reprieve is now needed to rescue Solinus from paralysis, Egeon from death, and the society of Ephesus from dissolution in madness, adultery, and incest. Clearly what is needed is the wonderful, restorative power of miracle. In desperation, the Duke summons the Abbess as witness to events. He turns literally and figuratively towards the Church, which at last delivers up its miracle: enter the Abbess with Antipholus and Dromio of Syracuse.

In a single moment of wonder Emilia's entry with the second Antipholus and Dromio resolves all the apparent discontinuity in Ephesus: instead of one Antipholus and Dromio, there are two; and all the misunderstandings and mistakings suddenly appear in their true form, as misunderstandings and mistakings merely, rather than as indications of witchcraft, madness, or adultery. At last the playwright reveals to his characters the secret he has shared with his audience since the second scene. And in the process he partly dissolves, at least for a moment, the distance between audience and characters, for when Emilia enters with the second Antipholus and Dromio, all the characters, struck dumb with wonder, become an audience to the revelations played out before them. And as characters become temporarily an audience, Shakespeare's audience may recognize that this situation is reversible – that an audience may be transformed into characters by a world more expansive than the one the playwright creates. After all, the revelations of the comic ending, by resolving the complications of the plot, remind the audience that the play is coming to an end; and one of the effects of such a reminder is to draw attention to the contracted nature of the audience's immediate experience. As they watch the play being concluded, the members of Shakespeare's audience may become aware that they must shortly surrender their perspective of godlike superiority and enter again a world where they themselves are characters. In this world, too, they may, like the characters of the play, be assailed by apparently discontinuous experience and perhaps observed by an audience which, from its godlike perspective, sees a comedy of errors in their fruitless efforts to understand a seeming discontinuity, whose meaning cannot be discovered without revelation.

In Shakespeare's manipulation of his audience's perspective here we find him again self-consciously playing with both his medium and his audience: using his medium to reflect back to the members of his audience an image, assimilated and reshaped, of their own condition; using his audience's awareness that the play draws towards its end to prepare its members for their return to a wider world. And, as a way of reminding the audience that its immediate world has been limited, in spite of the fact that it has temporarily experienced the illusion of a godlike perspective, Shakespeare dissolves that perspective. He plays with the audience's self-assurance about its understanding of events in *The Comedy of Errors* by reminding that audience, in the most obvious way, of its essentially limited perspective: he shocks his audience, as he shocks his characters, with a wondrous revelation – that Emilia is wife to Egeon and mother to the Antipholuses. The information is outrageous and ridiculous; it is also miraculous and wonderful, of a piece with the only other event quite like it in Shakespearean drama, the resurrection of Hermione. For in that moment, too, Shakespeare reveals to his audience a secret he has kept hidden from all, and audience and characters experience miracle and wonder together. Here, though, the tone of the revelation is more obviously playful than in *The Winter's Tale*, for Emilia, in revealing her identity, almost steps out of the action of the play to announce the playwright's exuberant delight in his powers. In the world of a play *anything* is possible: all characters and events serve the playwright's purposes as he suits them to the ordering form of his plot. Then, too, such an obvious manipulation of the dramatist's play world emphasizes the absoluteness of his powers over his audience, which can still be as suddenly surprised by the play as the characters are. And finally, and perhaps most importantly, Shakespeare here does what Solinus earlier could not do: he plays with discontinuity, suiting it to his purposes – and so reshaping it into the effectively coherent form of his plot – instead of merely pushing it aside. By playing with discontinuity, he transforms what is ridiculous to what is wonderful; out of manipulation, he makes miracle.

From one perspective Emilia's revelation offers yet one more example of discontinuity in this play world. How can she have been separated from her son and still live in the same town with him? Where has she been during the past twenty-five years? And why has she never revealed herself to Antipholus of Ephesus, who carries the name of her lost son and is served by a bondman named Dromio? Though an audience might not ask itself these particular questions – since they take us clearly beyond the boundaries of the play and precariously close to the state of mind that once found profit in exploring the girlhood of Shakespeare's heroines[7] – that audience *would* find Emilia's revelation preposterous, altogether discontinuous with her previously established identity as Abbess. But from another perspective, the miraculous revelation is both natural and coherent: since the action of *The Comedy of Errors* has driven its characters inevitably and predictably to this moment of pairing, to this public bringing together of all who have formerly been separated, the reunion of Egeon and Emilia becomes almost a thematic necessity. Though that reunion may seem logically ridiculous, discontinuous with the details of the play as we know them, it is at the same time thematically coherent, consistent with the patterns of the play as they are revealed to us. Emilia's appearance in the role of wife and mother, then, proves miraculous in two ways. Within the world of the play it offers wonderful resurrection and return; within the microcosm of the theater, it gives evidence of the dramatist's all-encompassing creative powers, which enable him, in making the ending of his play, to assimilate the particulars of logical discontinuity by fitting them to the patterns of overall thematic coherence.

Shakespeare's assimilation of discontinuity at the end of *The Comedy of Errors* also returns us, with a new perspective, to the concerns of the opening scene and of comedy in general – that is, to the problem of how to order the welter of human experience, filled as it is with missed opportunities, mistakes, forgettings, losses, and misjudgments, into a pattern that is both coherent and life-affirming. For comedy assures us that though our life may be tied inevitably to death, to loss, loneliness, and isolation, we may yet find an indefinite reprieve from such ontological disorder in temporary stays against confusion, in friends, family, and community. Such reprieves are, of course, always temporary, since, as Egeon's tale in the first scene shows, they all inevitably dissolve, sometimes even without warning, before the forces of time and tide; but they are, variously, reprieves nonetheless, and the best that man can do in the face of nature's arbitrary, apparently unyielding laws. All of which brings us back to Solinus and his problem in the first scene – and to the relationship between his action and Shakespeare's: the Duke's reprieve of Egeon's sentence here serves as a kind of dramatic emblem for the action of Shakespeare's play itself, since both offer insulated worlds of temporary relief from the harsh laws of intrusive reality. And the insulated world Solinus creates for Egeon – 'I'll limit thee this day/ . . . Try all the friends thou hast in Ephesus' (I. i. 151–3) – becomes for the audience the comedy of errors which fills up the time between Egeon's exit under temporary reprieve and his re-entry on the way to execution.

Of course there is a manifest difference between Solinus' reprieve of Egeon and the reprieve Shakespeare offers his audience. Solinus is throwing up a kind of desperate defense against a real and imminent threat to life, while Shakespeare is merely playing with the disorder threatening life. The play world he creates is doubly insulated against the intrusions of reality, since his Ephesus is an imaginative construct contained within the wider imaginative construct of the theater itself, while Solinus' temporary reprieve of Egeon is immediately circumscribed by the press of reality. But in a more general way the action of Shakespeare's comedy provides its audience with a reprieve not unlike that which Solinus offers Egeon. The members of Shakespeare's audience, attending a play, temporarily put aside their own problems, frustrations, and sorrows. They enter the theater, there to be entertained, and so to escape, for the space of an afternoon, the often harsh and arbitrary laws of nature and society which hold sway over their lives. The parallel is not, by any means, exact. Egeon is delivered from immediate execution, while Shakespeare's audience, if it thinks on death at all, views it from a great distance; no one ever went to a comedy for the express purpose of delaying his execution. But an audience which attends a 'comedy of errors' at least partly goes to the theater in order to find temporary reprieve from the problems of everyday life. Against such problems the play provides refuge by transporting that audience for a time to a realm of imaginative play – to an Ephesus shaped by Shakespeare's self-delighting dramatic powers.

Partly, too, the play offers its audience a reprieve from tragedy by its content as well as its context. The dominant sorrow and woe of the first scene quickly yield to the humorous mistakings and misunderstandings of the scenes which follow, and it is not long before Egeon's tragic story is, perhaps quite literally, forgotten. Shakespeare announces the advent of unmitigated comedy in this play by using a technique he will later employ almost unchanged in *The Taming of the Shrew*: he writes a second beginning which is essentially a revised version of the first, but very different in tone. In it many of the potentially tragic themes of Egeon's story are restated and reviewed through the perspective glass of comedy.

The second scene begins with a reference to the problem which has been the dominant concern in the Egeon episode, the law forbidding Syracusians to come to Ephesus; but where in the first scene that law was incontrovertible, binding even a ruler to its harsh dictates, here it is something that can be circumvented with ease: the traveler from Syracuse needs only to pretend that he is from Epidamnum. In this scene, then, we have clearly entered the realm of comedy, where laws are merely an inconvenience to be circumvented. Next we hear of Egeon, who has been the focus of our attention until now, but his story is put aside as easily as the law associated with it. The casual way in which Egeon's plight is dismissed may be a little surprising, since we have been led to believe in its dramatic importance, but the gesture of dismissal has obvious thematic purposes. First, it anticipates the ease with which the play itself will put aside Egeon's problems, since he is not to appear again until the last scene. And second, it presents a dramatic analogue of the audience's response to the same situation, because soon, like Antipholus of Syracuse here, the audience will become too absorbed in other business to give much thought to Egeon's plight.

It is a commonplace of criticism about *The Comedy of Errors* to argue that the tone of sadness established in the first scene is never really dispelled until the happy conclusion, that the perils of Ephesus as imagined by Antipholus of Syracuse are set in contrast to the real peril of Egeon there.[8] And this argument is undoubtedly true – but incomplete, because it does not stress the fact that the effect it describes is essentially subconscious. For it is perhaps even more true of an audience's response to this play to say that Egeon is soon forgotten and only returned to memory with his entrance in the fifth act. The reason for this effect is obvious: Shakespeare, playing with his audience's expectations and responses, directs attention away from Egeon. He puts almost a whole play between Egeon's first exit and his next appearance, and he radically alters the tone of the work in the meantime, filling it with all manner of laughable comings and goings. In addition, he releases his audience from worry about Egeon in the second scene, where first the problems raised by his plight are set aside and then the humorous confusion of comic mistaking begins.

Another melancholy merchant from Syracuse in search of his lost family arrives in Ephesus, but he is not threatened by the law that rigorously holds Egeon in bondage – he has only to declare himself of Epidamnum in order to walk freely about – and he is generously supplied with the commodity most valued in Ephesus and, sadly, unpossessed by the other merchant: money. He is also, as we can guess, one of Egeon's missing sons. And when, soon after the scene begins, he is mistaken for another Antipholus by a matching Dromio, we know that what Egeon has lost will soon be found again. That moment of mistaking is important for other reasons also. It finalizes the transformation begun in the play's opening speech, because it converts a potentially tragic situation to comedy by presenting apparent inconsistency of behavior in a humorous rather than a serious context. Here, too, the arbitrary violence of nature and society, so destructive and divisive in Egeon's view of experience, is reduced to comic form, as a slapstick beating and the subject of jokes:

> I have some marks of yours upon my pate,
> Some of my mistress' marks upon my shoulders,
> But not a thousand marks between you both.
> If I should pay your worship those again,
> Perchance you will not bear them patiently. (I. ii. 82–6)

But the most important function of this moment of mistaking is to turn the perspective glass of comedy upon the potentially tragic problem of discontinuity in human experience – a problem which, given comic form in this scene, becomes the organizing theme of the play. For from the time when Dromio of Ephesus mistakes Antipholus of Syracuse for his master until the time when the two sets of twins finally confront one another, characters are baffled, frightened, frustrated, and nearly maddened by a long series of experiences discontinuous with what they know to be the order of things. Antipholus of Syracuse, a stranger to Ephesus, is treated by Ephesians as if he had lived there all his life; Antipholus of Ephesus, who has spent his life establishing a reputation for honesty 'Second to none that lives here in the city' (v. i. 7), is accused of being a liar and a cheat; Dromio of Ephesus, a poor and faithful servant, is twice accused of stealing enormous sums of money; Dromio of Syracuse, following his master about a strange town, is claimed as a husband by a kitchen wench, all grease, whom he has never seen before and hopes never to see again. Adriana, trying to convince her husband to return home for dinner, is treated as a stranger by him; and Luciana, lecturing her brother-in-law on his duties to his wife, is answered by claims that he is unmarried and in love with her, not her sister.

What Shakespeare is here making laughable by his skilful manipulation of two sets of identical twins is only a ridiculous and exaggerated form of the inconsistency of ordinary human behavior and conduct. All men at different times put on different personalities;[9] and although very few of us have to live with the circumstance of repeatedly being mistaken for our identical twin, we all have known the embarrassing experience of being confused with someone else or of not being recognized by someone who should know us. Life is not altogether consistent or coherent in spite of our efforts to make it that way, and it is the incoherence, the discontinuity, of life that Shakespeare makes the subject of comedy in *The Comedy of Errors*. That is why he plays in this work not only with two confused sets of identical twins but also with man's abiding concern for time, money, and law. For all three – time, money, and law – provide man with an artificial but generally effective way of ordering inchoate experience; all three give him the illusion of constancy in a world of flux. Time is as regular as clockwork and as coherently patterned as yesterday, today, and tomorrow. Money is a sign of man's trust in at least one continuing system of values.[10] Law is a measure of his trust in his society. And all three, if they are to have meaning for man, must retain some measure of constancy, of stability.

This stability, however, is always partly illusory, because values are subjectively affected by experience. The thousand marks that Antipholus of Syracuse thinks it annoyingly inconvenient to lose are for Egeon his very life; an afternoon is a long time for Adriana to wait for her husband to return for dinner, but it is a short time indeed for Egeon to find a thousand marks in a strange city; and the law of Ephesus which not even the ruling Duke can countermand, a visiting sightseer can effortlessly circumvent. Life recalcitrantly resists' the continuity man, with his limited vision and understanding, would impose on it. And sometimes that resistance creates tragedy: Egeon cannot initially reconcile his sense of what life has given him with what it has taken away. But sometimes, too, that resistance creates comedy: Antipholus of Syracuse, repeatedly resolving to escape from the sorcery of Ephesus, becomes more and more entangled in its witchcraft, until miraculously his lost and wandering family is found and reunited – delivered from isolation and sorrow, and reborn, as Emilia's language makes clear, into the joy· of life together.

This final togetherness, characteristic of the inclusiveness of comic endings in general, provides a dramatic and thematic reflection of Shakespeare's technical mastery of, and delight in, his medium in *The Comedy of Errors*. As characters, apparently discontinuous in their behavior, at last are brought together and delivered into the wholeness of family and secured community, so also dramatic forms and formulas, seemingly discontinuous in their relationship, are ultimately brought together and assimilated into the wholeness of coherence and comedy in this play. Beginnings and endings, tragedy and comedy, farce and romance, laughter and sadness, logical impossibility and thematic necessity, characters and audience, predictability and surprise, mistake and miracle – all are made to serve the playwright's purposes and proclaim his powers as he shapes them into a 'comedy of errors' and coherent play, in both senses of the word.

2 'Form Confounded' and the Play of *Love's Labour's Lost*

Almost nothing about *The Comedy of Errors* prepares us for what we initially find in *Love's Labour's Lost*. From a play built almost entirely of plot and modelled on Plautine patterns of comedy, we move now to one built almost exclusively of language and modelled on the courtly dramas of John Lyly,[1] as if Shakespeare were consciously experimenting with a different form of stage comedy – which is almost certainly what he is doing. In *The Comedy of Errors* Shakespeare exuberantly celebrates his powers as a maker of dramatic plots; here he celebrates his powers as a maker of dramatic language. So if in the first of these comedies the characters often seem like puppets, guided through carefully choreographed movements by the hand of the playwright, in the second, the characters appear at times almost like ventriloquist dummies, deriving their life not so much from what they do as from what they say as they speak, in various voices and accents, the words of their master. In place of the puppets' persistent movement, they offer constant talk; in place of action, declamation. But *The Comedy of Errors* is not the only Shakespearean play whose structure is at odds with that of *Love's Labour's Lost*. Almost all of the comedies differ from it in at least one significant way. For when we think of comic action in Shakespearean drama, we think of near tragedy and of violence often just barely averted – of Egeon's sentence of death, of Shylock's pound of flesh, of Hero's 'death,' of Orsino's threat to kill what he loves, of Duke Frederick deciding to put his brother to the sword, of Oliver's plan to burn Orlando's lodging with him in it, of Demetrius and Lysander striking out with swords at one another, of old Vincentio haled and abused while threatening to torture Tranio. No such violence, though, appears in *Love's*

35

Labour's Lost, because the world of this play is carefully insulated against pain. In it there are no tyrannical parents to run from, no violence provoked by misunderstanding or malignant wrong-doing, no apparent madness or witchcraft affecting human behavior and threatening the very order of things. Instead characters engage in the ordinary, everyday activities of courtly life: they talk, they play games, they receive visitors, they hunt, they fall in love, they write letters and love poems, they put on a masque, and they watch a play. No Shakespearean comedy is so obviously free of violence and potential tragedy as *Love's Labour's Lost*. It is true that hints of such complications occasionally appear in the play: the King of Navarre proclaims a law which would treat men who keep company with women almost as harshly as the laws of Ephesus treat Syracusians; the pageant of the Worthies is disrupted by potential violence; and Mercade brings sudden, shocking news of death. But these possible complications are not darkly developed: the king begins to make exceptions to his law almost as soon as it is proclaimed; the violence at the pageant is all verbal; and Mercade's message comes suddenly, unexpectedly, from the world outside Navarre and, as we shall see, almost from outside the play. Navarre itself remains basically insulated from the violence, madness, and potential tragedy of other Shakespearean comedies.

Within its sheltered park and court the young men (no one apparently grows old in Navarre) pass their hours in play-making that is primarily verbal: writing laws, swearing oaths, building a great academe all of words, composing love letters and poems, rationalizing forsworn oaths, courting the ladies of France, preparing suitable dramatic entertainment for these ladies, and verbally baiting their social inferiors. In short, they inhabit the most insulated world in Shakespearean comedy – or in almost any other comedy before W. S. Gilbert's, for that matter. Their life is almost entirely free of work, study (in spite of their elaborate plans), parental authority, responsibility, monetary concerns, or sorrow. Not even the Forest of Arden, which is the closest equivalent to Navarre in Shakespearean comedy, is as sheltered as this world. For Arden has the melancholy Jaques to remind the Duke of his role as usurper; and immediately outside of Arden villains, planning to kill their brothers, prepare to disrupt its pastoral serenity. No one, however, is melancholy for long in Navarre, and the world outside is so easily forgotten that Mercade's entrance and message of death come as one of the most shocking surprises in Shakespearean drama.

So insulated, in fact, is the world of this play that we feel the presence of the playwright as conspicuously here as in *The Comedy of Errors*, though this effect is achieved in a very different way. Here Shakespeare does not proclaim his unbounded delight in his medium by obviously manipulating his characters and outrageously overgoing the limits of a credible plot line. Instead he calls attention to his play-making powers, as a dramatist celebrating the possibilities the theater offers his creative energies, by presenting a dramatized image of that sheltered world. Within the world of the theater, temporarily set off in time and place from the press of reality outside it, Shakespeare presents his audience with a dramatic world sheltered from the 'reality' of work, responsibility, sorrow, and death. As a playwright, working within the insulated world of the theater, his own action thus serves in some ways as the subject of his play – in which surrogate playwright figures, living within the sheltered world of Navarre, self-consciously construct their own staged productions principally by manipulating language in order to shape reality to their desires. As always in Shakespearean comedy, these correspondences appear not as equations, but as analogies. Neither the King of Navarre nor Berowne is to be closely equated with Shakespeare, and building an academe out of language or staging a masque of Muscovites is not the same thing as writing a play like *Love's Labour's Lost*. But between the young men of Navarre and Shakespeare there are notable correspondences, as there are between the king's creation of an academe and Shakespeare's construction of *Love's Labour's Lost*. Before examining these correspondences, however, we need to look once again at the insulated quality of this dramatic world, particularly as it contrasts with the chaotically disrupted world of *The Comedy of Errors*.

In place of Ephesus, rife with the comings and goings of tradesmen whose daily life is rigorously bound to the order and arbitrariness of time, law, and money, Shakespeare gives us in Navarre a kingdom 'Still and contemplative in living art' (I. i. 14) – if not of academe, at least of pastoral.[2] All the commonwealth of Navarre, as it appears in this play, is an enclosed and cultivated park, playground for the idle king and his attendant

lords, who find there deer to hunt, swains to laugh at, and ladies
to love. Unlike the inhabitants of Ephesus, no one in Navarre,
during the course of the play, ever works. Holofernes may have
pupils, but we never see them; Jaquenetta, turned over to the
custody of Constable Dull and ordered to become a dairymaid,
very quickly puts away dairying and the constable for dalliance
and Costard; and Nathaniel may get his living as a curate, but we
never see him administering to the needs of his parish. Everyone
in Navarre is on holiday, busily engaged in the manifold forms of
play, from love-making to fool-baiting, offered within the
round of the king's verdant park, and Shakespeare's wooden O.

Here even the business of ruling a kingdom can be playfully
pushed aside. The king begins by announcing that for the next
three years he will pursue the life contemplative – as if a king
were really free to abandon the worldy concerns of his kingdom.
Then when the unavoidable duties of rule do interrupt Navarre's
plans for a perfect academe, he gives the problems only the most
casual attention, consigning Costard the lawbreaker to the
keeping of Armado and throwing away Aquitaine for half of
what it is worth as surety. And this latter action, arising out of the
only real business of kingship demanding Navarre's attention in
the play, is of so little concern to him, and everyone else, that we
hear about it only as an afterthought in the fifth act, when the
Princess, called suddenly away by her father's death, summarily
thanks Navarre 'For my great suit so easily obtain'd' (v. ii. 749).

Problems of abiding concern in Ephesus, where people
struggle with the tyrannous inflexibility of their own constructed
systems of time, money, and law, have little place in the holiday
world of Navarre. There time repeatedly shifts its shape to suit
the dictates of human desire: a lifetime in pursuit of fame may be
as short as 'this present breath' (I. i. 5), three years' study as brief
as 'an hour' (I. ii. 39), or the latest minute of an hour time enough
for a king to consider making 'a world-without-end bargain' in
(v. ii. 799). Even the time scheme of the play shifts as we view it.
The action seems to consume most of two early summer
afternoons, but the imagery of the work suggests a much more
expansive temporal movement, from spring with its 'envious
sneaping frost/That bites the first-born infants . . .' (I. i. 100–101),
through summer when 'the cool shade of a sycamore' (v. ii. 89)
offers relief from afternoon heat, to a winter season of 'frosts and
fasts' (v. ii. 811), of 'speechless sick' (861), and of wretches

groaning 'in the throat of death' (865) – a pattern which is recapitulated, in a very different tone, in the haunting final song. Then, too, the world of *Love's Labour's Lost* is almost as free of concern about money and law as it is about time. The king has only the most casual interest in the two hundred thousand crowns he thinks he is owed by France. And the young lords, in bestowing rich gifts upon their loves, appear so prodigal that the ladies take this attention as merely 'courtship, pleasant jest and courtesy,/As bombast and as lining to the time' (V. ii. 790–1). For the common people of Navarre money is, of course, of more immediate interest than it is to the lords, but even for these people money is as much a subject for verbal as for material exchange. The poverty of his master regularly provides Moth with opportunities for mockery, and one of Costard's best comic speeches in the play explores the way in which language plays tricks with the intractable substantiality of money.

About the problem of law – man's laws, which are almost always in comedy arbitrary and something to be circumvented, usually at the end of the play by the action of the comedy as a whole – people in Navarre have no problem. There law is only a very temporary sort of inconvenience. We no sooner hear of the king's edict than we see its unworkability. Business of state brings the Princess of France to Navarre, and in negotiating with her about Aquitaine the king will of necessity have to disobey his own decree. 'Necessity,' Berowne reminds them, 'will make us all forsworn/Three thousand times within this three years' space' (I. i. 150–1), and he signs his name to the schedule of oaths while simultaneously talking of the excuses he will find for breaking faith. Then, as if to emphasize the validity of Berowne's perception, Costard is brought in as an offender against the edict. His defense of the naturalness of his crime – 'Such is the simplicity of man to hearken after the flesh' (I. i. 219–20) – is merely a more direct assertion of Berowne's earlier claim to 'like of each thing that in season grows' (107): in this world man cannot successfully legislate against the naturalness of sexual desire, nor does he really want to. Not even the king can take his own law seriously, for although his proclamation has promised a year's imprisonment to any man taken with a wench, he sentences Costard only to a week's fasting on bran and water in the custody of Armado. It is little wonder then that in less than a day Armado suspends even this sentence, for if the king cannot bring himself to enforce the rigor of his laws, we can hardly expect his agent to take their enforcement seriously.

At the beginning of *The Comedy of Errors* law is set aside, too, but in a very different way and with different results. Solinus cannot bring himself to order Egeon's death, so he grants him a temporary stay of execution. He does not, however, like Navarre, radically alter the harsh punishment proclaimed by law: he does not revoke the sentence of death; he merely postpones it. To Shakespeare, not Solinus, falls the task of circumventing the laws of Ephesus. So in his second scene the playwright puts aside the apparently tragic mood of his beginning and begins again, this time in a self-consciously comic way. But throughout the mistakings and mistimings which follow, the threat of harsh law, though sometimes forgotten, is never completely allayed: characters are promised imprisonment for debt, turned over to the custody of a jailer, and even thrown bound into a 'dark and dankish vault' (*Err.* v. i. 247). Then, near the end of the play, Egeon appears again, on his way to execution, and although we know that the sentence of death will not be exacted – that the characters, mere pawns of the playwright, are all at last being brought together so that they may be delivered from the harsh rigors and arbitrariness of law in Ephesus – the characters themselves have no such knowledge. They still think they live under Ephesian law.

In Navarre no one is ever threatened by the harsh laws of the land, for almost anyone can put them aside. Berowne scoffs at them; the king revises them as 'necessity' dictates and enforces them as common sense demands; Costard ignores them; Armado forswears them; and by the third act everyone but the Princess has apparently forgotten them. And she mentions them only to show the king that he has never taken his laws, or his oaths, seriously. The restraints imposed by law, time, and money, then, little affect life in Navarre's kingdom of play. And such problems as they do produce belong properly to others, from a world outside Navarre, where a king may fall into debt fighting wars, bind over part of his kingdom in surety for money borrowed, and then die before he has heard of its successful reacquisition. In the insulated world of Navarre, death – and the ultimate disorder it imposes on all human action – threatens man only from a very great distance, both physically and emotionally: it happens to someone who never appears in the play and who inhabits another realm, outside Navarre. So it can be known only by report.

To the young men of Navarre death is little more than a word, and they (unlike the ladies of France who come from the world outside the king's sheltered park) are at first no more emotionally affected by Mercade's message than they have earlier been by the king's talk of 'brazen tombs,' 'the disgrace of death,' and 'cormorant devouring Time' (I. i. 2–4). If the ladies would let them, they would continue their courtship uninterrupted, using this news of death as an excuse to move on to the next stage of wooing – betrothal – and so bring their play to a tidy conclusion. Near the end of *Love's Labour's Lost* the young men would repeat a pattern of behavior they have demonstrated before: they would confront a disruption and potential end to their play by talking it away, by linguistically manipulating it in such a way as to modify the description of their behavior, so that they can continue doing as they please. This is what they have done when they have earlier forsworn their vows of study in order to swear love to ladies who are 'the books, the arts, the academes,/That show, contain and nourish all the world . . .' (IV. iii. 352–3). And this is what the king tries to do again when he would facilely put away the Princess' sorrow, and the inconvenient interruption it poses to their game of love-making, by turning an aphorism to his advantage:

> . . . since love's argument was first on foot,
> Let not the cloud of sorrow justle it
> From what it purposed; since, to wail friends lost
> Is not by much so wholesome-profitable
> As to rejoice at friends but newly found. (V. ii. 757–61)

Such behavior from the king emphasizes again how insulated the inhabitants of Navarre are from sorrow and pain. They cannot really understand the Princess' sorrow because it comes to them indirectly: not in the unmediated action of experience – they have not, like Egeon, left the comfort of home to encounter a turbulent sea of sorrow, loss of loved ones, and imminent death – but in the mediating form of language – in their books they have encountered cliches about 'cormorant devouring Time,' and now Mercade softens his message of death as best he can. In the sheltered world of Navarre language often substitutes for the action of experience, perhaps because it substitutes for dramatic action as well. For no Shakespearean play is built so obviously out of words as *Love's Labour's Lost*.[3]

To be sure, words are the essential substance of *every* Shakespearean play, but not in quite the same way as in *Love's Labour's Lost*. Here words are as important as plot is in *The Comedy of Errors*: everywhere we look in Navarre, we find words calling attention to themselves; their importance is what we first notice about the play. Certainly there is little about the plot of *Love's Labour's Lost*, except perhaps its insubstantiality, which commands our attention.[4] The young men swear to establish an academe, forswear their oaths when they confront and court the ladies of France, and swear new ones when the ladies depart. During this time the lords and ladies encounter, and are entertained by, a group of commoners from Navarre and a thrasonical courtier from Spain, who also swears, forswears, and reswears oaths during the course of the play. It is almost as if Shakespeare, having written in *The Comedy of Errors* a comedy almost exclusively of plot, were here experimenting with one of virtually no plot at all. And what he uses to produce dramatic action in *Love's Labour's Lost* is language, particularly in its potentialities for play.

No one in Navarre can resist the impulse to play with words – to roll them trippingly off the tongue, to stab them rapier-like at an adversary, to pile them prominently in heaps of rhetorical passion, to twist them tortuously out of context, to turn them triumphantly to advantage. Most often this wordplay appears as punning – Molly Mahood counts over 200 examples in this, Shakespeare's most pun-filled work[5] – but it assumes a variety of other forms as well: jests, set speeches, oaths, malapropisms, sophistries, songs, aphorisms, sonnets, flatteries, conned embassages, and even an extemporary epitaph on the death of a deer. Such verbal pyrotechnics serve at least two purposes. First, they announce the playwright's self-conscious delight in his own, apparently unbounded, linguistic powers. Shakespeare is discovering in this play how dramatically useful his verbal facility can be – as a source of both character and action. And within the insulated world of the theater the playwright, like his characters within their sheltered park, plays tricks with language purely for the pleasure of exercising his own self-delighting powers. In this respect Shakespeare closely resembles his comic hero Berowne, who similarly exercises, and joys in, his almost unlimited verbal skills – which enable him, like the playwright, to assimilate the particulars of the insulated world around him and shape it to his desires. For Berowne, again like his creator, is an unusually gifted play-maker. His wit repeatedly shows itself in elaborate word-play; his bearing is that of an actor conscious that his friends regularly expect striking dramatic performances of him; and his imagination captures the potential dramatic elements of almost any situation, so that he cannot resist playing the role of rebel in the first scene, in spite of the fact that he intends all along to subscribe his name to the king's schedule for the perfect academe.

But there are also important differences between Berowne and Shakespeare, which direct us to a second purpose behind the linguistic facility of the characters in *Love's Labour's Lost*: that is, to call attention to the potential dangers of language irresponsibly used. Berowne's play, for instance, is almost entirely self-serving; he uses his manipulative skills with language in the service of his appetite – to steal center-stage from the king in the first scene, to convert self-confessed sexual desire into the appearance of idealistic love, to rationalize forswearing an oath he never meant to honor in the first place, and to abuse those who offer the Princess a pageant of Worthies in order to demonstrate the superiority of his own wit and dramatic imagination. The dangers of verbal facility, as they appear in Berowne, are obvious: such skills may nourish pride, hurt others, and serve as a means to distort truth, even when they are not consciously turned to villainous purpose. For Berowne's manipulation of language works to insulate him in a world of selfish satisfaction – and eventually perhaps of solipsism – by filtering experience through the distorting medium of words no longer grounded in objective reality. He would play with reality perversely, twisting it out of recognizable shape in the process of assimilating it, because he would have the object world as manipulable as sounds upon his tongue:[6]

> The king he is hunting the deer; I am coursing myself: they have pitched a toil; I am toiling in a pitch, – pitch that defiles: defile! a foul word. (IV. iii. 1–3)

Linguistic facility as Berowne practices it, then, shows how fun – manipulating words for the sheer pleasure of exercising one's wit – can shade into perversity – manipulating words, and worlds, no longer grounded in reality; the real danger of Berowne's wit is that it enables him to turn the light of truth into nonsense: 'Light seeking light doth light of light beguile' (I. i. 77) and so dissolve any system of values external to the self.

Shakespeare does little more than hint at the possibility of Berowne's solipsism in *Love's Labour's Lost*, but he is careful to discourage close identification between himself and his witty and linguistically facile hero, by repeatedly presenting implicit dramatic criticism of Berowne: in the obviously irresponsible way he swears to his oath in the first scene; in his blatantly inconsistent view of Rosaline, whom he first criticizes for plainness and sexual promiscuity and then praises as a goddess; in his comic undoing at the end of the eavesdropping scene; in his facile justification for forswearing his oath of allegiance to Navarre's academe; in his rude and childishly demonstrative response to the pageant of the Worthies; and finally, in Rosaline's criticism of him as a man whose reputation for wit has been earned at the expense of those he mocks. Berowne's manipulation of language thus divorces words from fact and undermines the basic foundation on which human communication and community are built – a trust in shared meaning, in the unchanging significance of a word from one moment to the next, and in the consistent relationship between words and things.

Stage plays, too, are built on such foundations, because they call into being the temporary community of an audience with whom the playwright and actors communicate. And there can be no play without such a trust in shared meanings between playwright and audience. For if a character announces himself as Pompey, and the audience answers, 'You lie, you are not he' (V. ii. 550), the play is done, as Shakespeare demonstrates in the disrupted pageant of the Worthies. In presenting Berowne as a gifted manipulator of language and a facile play-maker, then, Shakespeare calls dramatic attention not only to the joy but also to the danger confronting the playwright who, like him, would shape within a sheltered world yet another world built almost entirely out of language: that language and the play it gives form to must be rooted in the wider world outside the theater. However insulated that dramatic world may be, however personal its reference of action, however self-delighting its language, it must eventually speak meaningfully to members of an audience about a realm they know, and in a language they understand. Its insulated world may be an imaginative construct, but it must not be nonsensically personal or arbitrary; it must suggest a world in some ways recognizably real. That is why Navarre is not completely insulated, why for all its freedom from sorrow, madness, and death, it is still in its own way threatened by the disordering press of reality – in the form of niggling but intrusive interruptions which repeatedly foil characters' attempts to discover or to impose continuity on their experience.

As an example, consider the characters' concomitant fascination and frustration with the written word in *Love's Labour's Lost*. Nearly everyone in Navarre who can read also turns his hand to writing, as if the protean power of words and the intrusive reality they limned might be curbed and contained, harnessed in manageable form, by being given substance 'in print' (III. i. 173): the king issues a proclamation; his companions sign their names to a schedule of studies; Armado sends a letter to the king accusing Costard of villainy; the Princess announces her arrival by letter; Boyet promises written acquittances of France's payment to Navarre's father; all the young lords compose love poems; Armado and Berowne write love letters; the lovers pen an embassage for Moth to deliver as prologue to their masque; Nathaniel and Holofernes write a pageant and a dialogue in praise of the owl and the cuckoo. The written word, however, proves almost as elusively protean in this play as the spoken word, for proclamations are violated, schedules of study forsworn, letters miscarried, embassages forgotten, and pageants interrupted. Of these failures to bring the word under the control of fixed form, the last is the most important, both because it in a sense contains all the others and because it provides a metaphor for the play as a whole – itself an interrupted pageant consisting of a series of other, lesser, interrupted pageants.

The play begins, for instance, with a pageant that is hardly started before it meets with interruptions. The king, having issued edicts and proclamations and drawn up a schedule of studies, has called his courtiers together to formalize the founding of his academy. To celebrate the occasion, he has even prepared a speech, a suitably sententious set-piece after the manner of a warrior before his troops. He talks of fame and honor, of the insignificance of life without great achievement, of the inevitability of death, and of the glory that can be won by those who seek to make Navarre 'the wonder of the world':

> Let fame, that all hunt after in their lives,
> Live register'd upon our brazen tombs
> And then grace us in the disgrace of death;
> When, spite of cormorant devouring Time,
> The endeavour of this present breath may buy ,
> That honour which shall bate his scythe's keen edge
> And make us heirs of all eternity.
> Therefore, brave conquerors, – for so you are,
> That war against your own affections ·
> And the huge army of the world's desires, –
> Our late edict shall strongly stand in force:
> Navarre shall be the wonder of the world;
> Our court shall be a little Academe,
> Still and contemplative in living art. (I. i. 1–14)

Here in sonorous, end-stopped regularity suggestive of Marlowe's mighty line is the expansive language of the Renaissance overreacher, grasping after knowledge infinite in an attempt to make himself the heir 'of all eternity'; here is a king self-consciously aspiring to the rhetorical power and pageantry of Tamburlaine. Navarre even once makes a veiled reference to a correspondence between his methods and Tamburlaine's: 'Our late edict shall strongly stand in force.'

The gravity of the king's purposes and pronouncements is, however, called into question from the very beginning of his speech. 'Fame,' his second word, has associations with rumor as well as with glory; and 'hunt,' his second verb, suggests as much an activity of play as of high-seriousness. Also, Navarre's easy dismissal of life as the mere 'endeavour of this present breath' is just too facile. It suggests that the king really has no conception of how difficult the task he sets for himself and his companions is. Such a suggestion is also enforced by the formulaic neatness of the speaker's references to the forces of death and time – 'Live register'd upon our brazen tombs,' 'grace us in the disgrace of death,' 'cormorant devouring Time,' 'That honour which shall bate his scythe's keen edge' – which emphasize that Navarre's experience of the threats these forces represent has so far been entirely literary. Finally, the seriousness of the king's declamation is undermined by the pretentiousness of its central metaphor: all his talk of war and armies and conquerors only draws attention to the fact that his proposed plan is not really for a battle in which man immediately confronts death, but for a study project given inflated importance by a young king with little else to do.

Ruler over a kingdom as serene as its insular park, Navarre has to find some outlet for his energies, so he conceives the idea of the academy, as he will later conceive the idea of love, with an extravagant totality of commitment. Nothing else apparently matters to him but study and the ideal community of scholars he will establish. He does not even make provisions for the rule of his kingdom; it will, he seems to think, take inspiration from the rarefied atmosphere of the court academy. The very excessiveness of Navarre's scheme, however, calls it into doubt, for like the similarly extreme plans of self-denial proffered by Lucentio and Olivia near the beginning of other Shakespearean comedies, it signals a clearly unrealistic view of human experience. It is obviously life-denying, and the character who proposes it is just as obviously life-affirming – young and guardedly receptive to the play of those around him. The energies he seeks to lock up will not long be contained.

For a time Navarre's pageant continues. Like Lear later, though in a very different mood from the old king, he stage-manages the scene of his announced retirement by calling upon his most important subjects to swear extravagant oaths of loyalty to him. And also like Lear, Navarre is answered first by two subjects who formulaically pledge their faith and then by a third who publicly resists, so interrupting the pageant as it has been planned by the king. First Longaville and then Dumaine promise to turn away from the world and the flesh in order to give banquet to the mind, and what is perhaps most notable about their vows is their rote, almost ritualistic quality, as if the two lords were merely repeating tidy speeches assigned to them, which in a sense is what they are doing. Berowne begins as formulaically as his predecessors: 'I can but say their protestation over' (33), but he very quickly turns formula to his particular advantage – 'Which I hope well is not enrolled there' (38, 46) – and disrupts Navarre's pageant. He does not, however, like Mercade later, bring a sudden halt to the action. What he does instead is to make the king's play over into his own: he seizes control of the dramatic situation and manipulates it so that he becomes the center of attention in a play that is then more his own than the king's. Upon the ruin of one interrupted play Berowne – and Shakespeare – constructs another, soon itself to be interrupted by the entrance of Costard.

To be sure, *all* plays are structured in something like this way, as one speech, exchange of dialogue, or scene succeeds another. But rarely in a drama does a playwright make the skeletal framework of his art as obvious as Shakespeare does in *Love's Labour's Lost*, where he regularly draws his audience's attention to interrupted plays and pageants.[7] A list of notable examples includes, besides Navarre's disrupted pageant of the first scene: the negotiations over Aquitaine, which are put off until the arrival of the packet of acquittances from France; the lovers' severally assumed stances of shock at their fellows for betraying their academy to love, which are each cut short by evidence of wrong-doing on the part of the accuser; the embassage of Moth and masque of the Muscovites, both disrupted by the mockery of the ladies; and the pageant of the Worthies, interrupted first by the rude remarks of the nobles, then by Costard's challenge to Armado, and finally by the arrival of Mercade. By presenting so many examples of failed drama, of 'form confounded' (V. ii. 520)[8] in this play, Shakespeare is bringing art into more immediate contact with life, dramatizing in the insulated world of Navarre as he creates it the challenge of that other insulated world of the theater as he confronts, and also creates, it. In making a play that repeatedly depicts the attempts of others to make *their* plays, Shakespeare here dramatizes again a theme which he has explored in a somewhat different way in *The Comedy of Errors* – that of the discontinuity of human experience.

In that play Egeon began by trying to impose on the discontinuous events of his life a pattern of tragic continuity. In a public confrontation with death, he tried to shape a narrative account of his life that would give it the form of an ordered tragedy, whose disastrous ending is implicit in its every detail. But the discontinuity of reality, which resisted the tidy continuity of his tragic story first skewed his narrative and then interrupted the prescribed order of two simultaneous public ceremonies – one an execution, the other a Shakespearean play. Within both the world and the structure of *The Comedy of Errors*, then, Shakespeare succeeds in doing what his characters cannot accomplish: he masters the intrusive discontinuity of life by gathering it into the ordered continuity of art. He begins with a similar problem in *Love's Labour's Lost*. Although the first scene of this play differs radically in mood from the beginning of *The Comedy of Errors*, Shakespeare again begins with a public confrontation of death – now viewed from the securely mediating distance of youth – and a character determined to impose a pattern of continuity on the intrusive press of reality – the young men of Navarre will dedicate themselves unremittingly to study and so establish a kind of absolute continuity in their lives. Again, too, as in *The Comedy of Errors*, details of the character's speech suggest an opposing complexity, and discontinuity, in events that the speaker overlooks. And finally, as in *The Comedy of Errors*, the ordered ceremony is hardly begun before it meets with an interruption that sets the tone for the play to follow and announces the playwright's successful dramatic assimilation of discontinuity within the insulated world of the theater. There is, of course, an important difference in tone between these two beginnings. One seems predominantly tragic, since Egeon is immediately threatened by death; while the other is clearly comic, since the young men of Navarre know death only as a word to be manipulated in the facile phrases of cliches. The worlds of Ephesus and Navarre are, as we have already noted, clearly disparate, even if Shakespeare's dramatic concerns in both plays are not so different as at first they may seem.

One important measure of the difference between the worlds of these plays is in what Shakespeare does with the theme of discontinuity in them. In *The Comedy of Errors* he was concerned primarily with the act of interpreting experience, of discovering a coherent pattern in the threateningly discontinuous events of everyday life. And behind the apparent disorder of things in Ephesus there appears at last a discernible order, coherent and miraculous, revealing itself to the characters and delivering them from the bondage of their own mistakings. The pattern may have been long hidden and elusive, discernible in part only by chance, but in Shakespeare's Ephesus there *is* a pattern of coherence – with a beginning, a middle, and an end – to be discovered. In Navarre there is no such pattern. In place of the carefully structured plot which orders the world of *The Comedy of Errors*, Shakespeare has provided a series of apparently

haphazard meetings between lords and ladies, lords and commoners, and ladies and commoners. These meetings are not, in
fact, altogether unmotivated (the characters do have things to say
to one another) or unpatterned (the scenes focus alternately on
the nobility and the common people), but they give no clear
impression of a single controlled and developing action, building
to a conclusion in time. Instead they suggest episodic events,
often interrupted and only loosely related. If Shakespeare in *The
Comedy of Errors* is giving dramatic emphasis to the difficulty of
interpreting experience that *seems* discontinuous, here he is
showing how man faces the difficulty of encountering experiences which *are* discontinuous, either psychologically or actually. In Navarre life does not ultimately reveal itself as a coherent
pattern, with a beginning, a middle, and an end; rather, it appears
as a series of interrupted actions out of which other actions must
then be begun: characters constantly meeting with disruptions
constantly attempt to overcome them with new beginnings.

Sometimes such disruptions are as insignificant and passing as
a thought or memory – the Princess pauses in the middle of the
hunt to meditate on fame; Katharine briefly interrupts her banter
with Rosaline to remember her sister's death. Sometimes,
though, the disruptions are more significant and lasting – their
love for the ladies forces the king and his companions to abandon
their idealistic plans for an academe; their rudeness publicly
humiliates a group of vain but well-intentioned commoners
during the pageant of the Worthies. And occasionally, the
disruptions are so consequential and complete as to alter the
course of a life – the news of Jaquenetta's pregnancy prompts
Armado to turn away from the court and follow the plow;
Mercade's announcement of France's death interrupts the love-
games of the nobles and provokes vows of year-long retreats, by
the Princess into mourning, by Navarre into a monastery, and by
Berowne into a hospital. Whatever the nature of the disruptions,
however, they suggest the inseparable entanglement of beginnings and endings in life, which as we live it, and as it is presented
in the world of *Love's Labour's Lost*, consists of an endless series of
actions begun, interrupted, and either begun again or abandoned for the beginnings of new actions. In the process
expectations, both great and small, often remain unfulfilled –
the king's scheme to make Navarre 'the wonder of the world'
collapses with the arrival of the ladies from France; his plans for

an afternoon masque to entertain them are upset by the ladies' mockeries. And behind the failures of such expectations, behind the sudden, unlooked-for endings of such high-minded beginnings, life is shadowed by the threat of incoherence and discontinuity, by the inevitable and ultimate interruption of grand beginnings:

> The sweet war-man is dead and rotten; sweet chucks, beat not the bones of the buried: when he breathed, he was a man. (v. ii. 666–8)

Such a view of life does not necessarily, as it seems, negate the more optimistic vision of *The Comedy of Errors*; the two plays may merely be offering the same view from different perspectives. Life, fraught with the apparently ceaseless intrusion of endings upon beginnings, may contain an ordered pattern of coherence – beginnings passing through middles to endings – as yet unrevealed to those who, living within the larger framework of such a pattern, notice only the disruptions that regularly put an abrupt end to their best beginnings. In *The Comedy of Errors*, after all, the characters do not know until the end that their mistimings and mistakings are all part of a carefully controlled and perfectly coherent action, operating both within their world and above it. They do not know either that there are two sets of Antipholuses and Dromios, who are being confused, or that they are characters in a play. The real difference of perspective between these two plays, then, extends not to the characters but to the audience. For we very soon know how the action of *The Comedy of Errors* will end, but we are, as much surprised as the characters by the denouement of *Love's Labour's Lost*.

Secure in the knowledge that comes with our perspective of superiority over the characters – since we *do* know that they are only persons in a play – we observe their failures and embarrassments with bemused delight. Like Berowne in his tree, we sit like demi-gods in the sky and enjoy the comedy being played before us, taking pleasure in our heightened perspective, which enables us to know things that the characters do not: that the youthful enthusiasm of the lords will not be long bound to the rigors of academe, that their masque will be mocked, and that they swear vows of love to the wrong ladies. But also like Berowne in the tree, we may become too confident of our unassailability; so Shakespeare, after playing with our self-assurance as audience, brings us metaphorically back to earth, where we can be surprised by sudden and unsuspected events: enter Mercade in black, to interrupt the merriment. For a moment the action comes to a complete – I am tempted to say 'dead' – end. The quarrel between Armado and Costard is cut off, the laughter and jesting subside, and as Mercade prepares to deliver his unspeakable message, we and the characters simultaneously confront the one ending unimaginable in this, the most talk-filled of Shakespeare's plays – utter silence: 'The king your father – ' (v. ii. 728). Abruptly the processes of life, and of the play, come to a stop, as death casts its shadow across the stage of both the characters' lives, and ours: 'Dead, for my life!' (729).

The moment is strikingly surprising, perhaps unique in Elizabethan drama[9] – a sudden, wrenching change of tone that disrupts not only the entertainment of the lords and ladies but also the security of the audience, which is reminded with dramatic suddenness of its own vulnerability to Mercade's shattering message. For the past two hours this audience, delighting in the entertainment Shakespeare has provided, has been able to forget that it is really no more secure in the insular world of its theater than the characters of *Love's Labour's Lost* are in Navarre's park. The play proceeding in both worlds can, at any moment, be interrupted by the entrance of Mercade, messenger of death – the most disruptive of all unlooked-for endings. Mercade's appearance here, although it has no clear precedents in the Elizabethan theater, does, however, have distant analogues both in medieval drama, when the figure of death precipitously summons a sinner to his doom,[10] and in epic poetry, when a messenger of the gods descends to man. In each of these cases man, both within the work of art and outside it, stands briefly at 'the intersection of time and the timeless'[11] and looks upon what is eternal. In *Love's Labour's Lost* the eternal appears in the guise of the 'real,' the harsh fact of death breaking in upon the nobles' insubstantial entertainment. But the news of death arrives as from another world – Mercade materializes suddenly,[12] like a figure sent from the heavens. And what he is sent to reveal is the insubstantiality of *all* human entertainment. Watching characters in a play who are interrupted as they watch characters in a play, we cannot fail to notice the correspondence between the play world and our own: we, too, watchers in one play, may be participants in another, shaped by a playwright who at any moment may dispatch his messenger of death to interrupt our fun.

Further intensifying our awareness of the correspondence between the players' world and ours is the fact that Shakespeare has just finished showing us an audience rudely unreceptive to the pageant being staged before it, as if to ask us for a more sympathetic, intelligent response than the Worthies receive from the nobles. When the commoners perform before them, the king and his companions are unwilling to grant the players even the necessary courtesy of accepting their fictive roles. From the first, they are disruptive:

> I Pompey am,–
>> You lie, you are not he! (v. ii. 550)

As a result the pageant fails to communicate its theme to its audience, whose members are too much concerned with repairing their own damaged reputations in the present to be interested in men of reputation from the past. More important, this audience of nobles in its vanity is so self-involved that it fails to be affected even by moments of genuine human feeling and sympathy which occasionally break through the shabbiness of the pageant and put these ridiculous Worthies momentarily in touch with what in man *does* make him worthy – his capacity for compassion and community: 'There, an 't shall please you; a foolish mild man; an honest man, look you, and soon dashed. He is a marvellous good neighbour, faith, and a very good bowler: but, for Alisander, – alas, you see how 'tis, – a little o'erparted' (v. ii. 585–9). We as audience may be moved by what only amuses these vain and foolish noblemen, and we may as a result feel the presence of the playwright asking for our needed tolerance and compassion, as he presents his pageant before us. Our sensitivity to the precariousness of human endeavor may thus be intensified just before Mercade enters, to remind us of the insubstantiality of *our* pageant.

But although Mercade's entrance brings an end to the commoners' play and, in a sense, interrupts Shakespeare's, it does not finally end *Love's Labour's Lost*. In this drama of grand beginnings that are repeatedly disrupted by unlooked-for endings Shakespeare follows the examples of his characters and builds a new beginning on the ruins of the old one. He concludes his play by turning his characters, as well as his audience, out into a world wider than the insulated confines of the theater. For when the ladies of France impose trials upon their lovers to test the validity of sworn vows, their intent is not only to separate their lovers from the company of former playmates;[13] it is also to force the young men out of the king's sheltered park, where these lords have been free to play at being 'boy eternal' (*The Winter's Tale*. I. ii. 65), and into a world of time, where the possibility of their growth is tied also to the inevitability of decay and death:

>   . . . then, if sickly ears,
> Deaf'd with the clamours of their own dear groans,
> Will hear your idle scorns, continue then,
> And I will have you and that fault withal;
> But if they will not, throw away that spirit,
> And I shall find you empty of that fault,
> Right joyful of your reformation. (v. ii. 873–9)

The young men's facile vows of love can have meaning for their ladies only if those men can be thought capable of moving beyond their world of 'living art,' only if they are willing to leave the insulated perfection of the king's park behind them. There the art they have been living has closed out too much of life. Mistakenly beginning with the thought that they can separate the gross particulars of life from their exclusive pursuit of knowledge, the young men have quickly fallen into a second kind of error: they have separated life from love, for their courtship of the ladies from France is no less artificial than their original plans for a perfect academe.[14] As lovers the young men are merely living the art of love-making as it appears in Renaissance literature. In fact, so conventional and unindividualized are their protestations of love – in letter, in sonnet, in masque, and in conversation – that we cannot tell one lover or loved one from another, and neither can the men, as their foolish mistaking during the masque proves. It is no wonder, though, for in all the praise of the young ladies there is hardly a word of what they *look* like: we know that Rosaline is dark, and almost nothing else – except that the Princess is heavier than any of her attendants, a fact which comes to us from Costard, not from the lovers. One reason why we know so little about what the ladies look like is because the young men never really see them as particularized women, only as convenient objects upon whom to project their conventionalized notions of love. And that love, as the king's sonnet to the Princess makes clear, is almost entirely *self*-centered:

> Thou shinest in every tear that I do weep:
> No drop but as a coach doth carry thee;
> So ridest thou triumphing in my woe.
> Do but behold the tears that swell in me,
> And they thy glory through my grief will show:
> But do not love thyself; then thou wilt keep
> My tears for glasses, and still make me weep. (IV. iii. 33–9)

From this self-centered vision of love, product of a narrowly oversimple and conventionalized understanding of how life may be shaped into 'living art,' the ladies of France seek finally to deliver their lovers. That is why the penances they impose will take the young men beyond the boundaries of the king's park and into a world where life never attains to ordered perfection.

These imposed trials will also take the young lovers beyond the boundaries of Shakespeare's play, both in time – 'a twelve-month and a day' (v. ii. 887) – and in place – 'To some forlorn and naked hermitage,/Remote from all the pleasures of the world' (v. ii. 805–6). In this way too the trials promise delivery from the insularity of 'living art,' in another sense of the phrase. Drama itself is, literally, living art, not only in being an art form that depicts life but also in using living actors for such depiction. Thus when Shakespeare at the end of *Love's Labour's Lost* has his characters draw attention to the artificiality of drama's conventionally tidy endings – 'Our wooing doth not end like an old play;/Jack hath not Jill . . .' (v. ii. 884–5) – he is making use of a convention in order to transcend it. Having disrupted our expectations about the way *Love's Labour's Lost* will end, Shakespeare then calls attention to this disruption: this play does not end like a play. The young lovers, so neatly and symmetrically matched, are not united in marriage. Instead the men must undergo trials to prove their worth, and faithfulness, to their ladies. And as they swear facile vows of constancy to their newly imposed tasks, these lords sound very like the foolishly self-assured young men who earlier found it so easy to swear to an extravagant three years' study project. This ending is, as a number of critics have pointed out,[15] just another conventional beginning, very like both the one that began this play and ones regularly associated with comedy in general, where young heroes often have to suffer through a series of trials before they can succeed in love.

Shakespeare ends *Love's Labour's Lost* with a beginning for a number of reasons. First, the young men of Navarre, though at the end of a play, are also at the beginning of a new experience, which promises to take them outside the narrow confines of the king's park and their own self-absorption. Second, the ending, by so closely recalling the beginning of the play, emphasizes the dubiousness of the men's new vows. The lords may think their constancy in trial is certain, but they may prove as faithless in love as in study. The ending of the lovers' story is thus shadowed in the unpredictabilities of life not only by being projected forward beyond the bounds of the play but also, paradoxically, by being directed backwards towards its beginning. Third, and most important, Shakespeare is here working with an effect that is a dominating concern of his comedies: he is breaking down the conventional barriers between his play and actuality, between actors and audience, between drama and life. Drama, after all, *is* life for a man who makes his living in the theater, writing and acting in plays and keeping company with other players and playwrights. And life often takes on the qualities of drama, since we all at times see ourselves as characters engaged in an action of some coherence, with a beginning, a middle, and an end. In the process other characters, coming and going around us, make their entrances and exits in our play.

However this may be, the conclusion of *Love's Labour's Lost* offers its characters, and its audience, the promise of all comic endings: that is, a dramatic celebration of man's *un*ending capacity to build new beginnings upon the broken remains of old ones. The world of Navarre may be one in which man's hopes – his great schemes and his little plans alike – come to nothing, but it is not a world in which anyone is easily discouraged or ultimately defeated. Mercade's message, after all, comes from a realm *outside* Navarre, and his appearance, though dark, is fleeting, only briefly suggesting the more imposing shadows which will later darken the worlds of the mature comedies and eventually take full-bodied form in *Hamlet*, –

another drama of academic study disrupted, of pageants interrupted, and of great beginnings crossed by unexpected endings.
In that play, though, the messenger bringing the news of a
father's death comes literally from another world and appears at
the beginning of the play. And the shadow he casts is not fleeting
but permanent, blackening the clothes and countenance and
thoughts of the hero, and taking him at last to the earthy stage of
man's inescapable end, where he can feel the worthless dust of all
human endeavor slip through his fingers. Such a vision, however, is a long way from the world of *Love's Labour's Lost*, where
Mercade enters and leaves almost in a moment and where human
failure produces at worst silence and embarrassment – Nathaniel
withdrawing from the pageant – and at best either a virtuoso
verbal performance – Berowne justifying the abandonment of
the academy – or a chance to begin again — the king swearing
new vows of constancy that make the ending of the play also a
beginning. In such a world even the best of beginnings may be
threatened by disruption; no spring is without the cuckoo's song
and the threat it poses to human relationships. And even the
worst of endings may provide opportunities for new beginnings;
winter, the season of death, sickness, and cold without, is also the
season of communal cooperation, merriment, and warmth
within.

3 Enter the Hero: The Power of Play in *The Taming of the Shrew*

It is hardly surprising at a time when critical energies aim insistently at classification that criticism of Shakespearean comedy should play a kind of shell game with *The Taming of the Shrew*: no matter which rubric of classification we look under, *The Taming of the Shrew* is not likely to be there. It is, we find from a number of recent studies, neither happy, pastoral, nor festive comedy[1] – even though it includes some of Shakespeare's funniest and fun-filled scenes; contains a journey to the country where the heroine, encountering stark images of her own condition, learns to play her way out of that condition; and dramatizes the actions of young men on holiday, as presented in play before the drunken unwatch of a lord of misrule. Neither, apparently, is *The Taming of the Shrew* an early 'metadrama,'[2] although it focuses almost as intensively as *A Midsummer Night's Dream* and *Richard II* upon man's actions as play and his identity as player. This critical confidence game of hide-*The-Taming-of-the-Shrew*, however, finds its most finished form in two recent studies of 'Early Shakespeare,' that ignore the play with barely a word of explanation.[3] Clearly, when we cannot find *The Taming of the Shrew* under 'Early Shakespeare,' we can hardly expect to find it anywhere,[4] and it is time to cry foul against a critical sleight of hand which has surreptitiously cast our play away among the scraps and leavings under the table.

Critics no doubt have reason to turn attention aside from *The Taming of the Shrew*. Criticism is built on text, and this text is suspect. With this play, more perhaps than with any other Shakespearean work, what we have seems hardly a just representation of what Shakespeare meant to write. The biggest problem certainly is the Induction, which first introduces characters who have nothing directly to do with the shrew-taming plot and then abruptly abandons them once the play proper is under way. This problem is then further compounded by the uncertain status of *The Taming of a Shrew*, which may be either a source or a bad quarto of Shakespeare's play, and which supplies an ending for the frame of the Induction.[5] Is this ending a part of Shakespeare's source which he strangely chose to ignore? Or is it a version of a lost ending Shakespeare originally wrote, as remembered by the compiler of the quarto? Or, finally, is it, like Baptista's third daughter in *The Taming of a Shrew*, perhaps merely the invention of a compiler determined to order and improve upon *his* source? Then, as if such insoluble problems of beginning and ending were not enough to discourage the critic, difficulties appear in the middle of the play as well. There Tranio's sudden transformation (in his guise as Lucentio) into Petruchio's old friend, Hortensio's precipitous and largely unmotivated decision to visit Petruchio's taming school, and Gremio's lack of interest in how Cambio, supposedly his agent, fares with Bianca suggest more than Shakespeare's occasional oversight of detail.[6] Such inconsistencies suggest incompletion, or the beginnings of radical revision. The play as we have it is almost certainly unfinished.

But the precarious state of its text is not the only reason why Shakespearean critics now so often exclude *The Taming of the Shrew* from discussions of the comedies. There is another, more obvious reason: the play just does not fit neatly into conventional modes of classification. Shakespeare, Northrop Frye has taught us, wrote essentially romantic New Comedy, works descended from Menander, Plautus, and Terence and distinguished by teleological plots in which an alienated lover moves toward sexual fulfilment, marriage, and a renewed society.[7] In a very general way *The Taming of the Shrew* follows this pattern. Petruchio, at first alienated from the heroine, devises a plan to win her, endures various trials in the process of securing her love, and ultimately triumphs by bringing forth his 'true' wife during a final recognition scene, staged at a wedding banquet. In the process the principal characters discover new identities and settle into new social roles. The only problem with such a general summary of *The Taming of the Shrew* is that it overlooks nearly everything of importance in the play: the rough outlines of a conventional New Comedy plot in the work serve principally to call attention to its *un*conventionality.

Most obviously, the hero is unconventional. He is a boaster, a brawler, a self-server, whose first action is to beat his servant and whose second is to announce himself intent upon making a moneyed marriage – conduct a little bold-faced for the hero of a New Comedy. His apparent plan for winning the heroine is also a strange departure from convention. First he launches into a courtship that, under cover of conventional lover's praise, is nothing less than psychological rape – as the predominance of sexual puns in the scene emphasizes. Then, having converted the ceremony of courtship to rape, he does the same thing with the ceremony of marriage, declaring his wife, with purposely obscene suggestion, 'household stuff' (III. ii. 233), tearing her at point of sword from her family, and carrying her off like mere cartable goods. Petruchio, though, is not the only one who perpetrates a kind of rape in this scene. Shakespeare himself also commits sudden and forcing violation here: he rapes convention.[8] For with his comedy barely half over he had married his hero and heroine.

True, they give little promise of living happily ever after, and the whole point of the wedding-rape is that it is hardly a wedding at all. A real marriage, one of true minds without impediment, has yet to be earned, and learned. That Petruchio is to teach Kate in a violently unconventional manner. She is put to the tests common to young lovers – flight from home, deprivation, violence, and threatening madness – but her oppressor is not fate, arbitrary law, or a tyrannous father; it is not even a scornful young man resisting her declarations of love. Instead it is an apparently half-crazed and all-too-solicitous husband. And Petruchio, for his part, suffers trials too – a long and arduous journey, disorder in the home, hunger, sleeplessness, and betrayal by those he loves. Only these trials are all self-made, strange fantasies of an apparently disordered mind.

In this madness there is reason, however, and Petruchio finally imposes his mad vision upon the world: Kate proves herself a loving wife at the final wedding banquet. And where earlier Bianca, the model child and apparently model wife-to-be, replaced Kate in the seat of honor at her marriage feast, now Kate metaphorically replaces Bianca, as the center of attention and virtue. Two acts before, the wedding feast of hero and heroine was interrupted before it could begin. Then the hero and author both seemed bent upon rape, but the play has proved them actually law-abiders in disguise: Petruchio has waited for the conclusion of this wedding feast to consummate his marriage – 'Come, Kate, we'll to bed' (v. ii. 184) – and Shakespeare has led his audience by an unfamiliar route back to the security of the ending it expects. By earlier displacing and disordering the marriage which traditionally concludes New Comedy, he has challenged the tyranny and shallowness of this convention only to return it at last, newly charged with meaning, to its accustomed place at the conclusion of the play. Like Petruchio, he has threatened rape but finally answered to the law's restraint.

Yet even when Petruchio and Shakespeare most obviously seem to rebel against convention in this play, they are actually falling back upon another, still older convention. Much that is not New Comedy in *The Taming of the Shrew* is Old Comedy. Petruchio, for example, would be an almost conventional hero in an Aristophanes play. 'In Aristophanes,' Cedric Whitman writes:

> the comic hero is a low character who sweeps the world before him, who dominates all society . . . creating the world around him like a god . . . [T]he comic hero himself is wayward, and abides by no rules except his own, his heroism consisting largely in his infallible skill in turning everything to his own advantage, often by a mere trick of language. He is a great talker.[9]

Like the heroes of Aristophanes, Petruchio touches upon the 'low,' the bestial, in man's nature. His language, often scurrilous, repeatedly suggests a life actively dominated by the senses. Eating, drinking, sleeping, kissing, fighting, hawking, hunting and money-grabbing are everywhere in his talk. Then to enforce his hero's tie to the bestial, Shakespeare has given Petruchio a servant who is his grotesque shadow figure, a petty tyrant and creature all of appetite. Petruchio is like the heroes of Aristophanes also in being a self-server. Almost as soon as he appears, he announces his self-interested purpose:

> Antonio, my father, is deceased;
> And I have thrust myself into this maze,
> Haply to wive and thrive as best I may: . . . (I. ii. 54–6)

I come to wive it wealthily in Padua;
If wealthily, then happily in Padua. (I. ii. 75–6)

Here is a bald-faced, fortune hunter sure, and no apparent concern for the niceties of conventional conduct or social decorum will blunt his desire for gain. Even the death of a father serves Petruchio to advantage: it puts money in his purse and frees him to venture for marriageable merchandise abroad. The self-interest is matched only by his enormous ego, which keeps him from ever doubting of success. That is Aristophanic too. But the characteristic which makes Petruchio most like the heroes of Aristophanes is his capacity to carry nearly all before him with the magic of his talk. As he moves through Padua, he talks the world into submission, remaking it according to his desires, almost as if he were a god.

He begins first by imperiously twisting language and Grumio's ears in an argument about the meaning of the word 'knock.' Then in announcing his intent to conquer Kate, he reduces her scolding tongue to the mere snapping of a chestnut in a farmer's fire. When next he meets the father of a bride-to-be, he quickly negotiates a self-aggrandizing, no-nonsense business deal and then readies himself for a verbal duel with Kate. The rest of the play catalogues his victories in this extended duel, as he transforms her insults to compliments, her contention to agreement, her rebellion to alliance, and ultimately her hate to love. Here, if anywhere outside of Aristophanes, is the *poneria*[10] of the Old Comic hero.

It is no wonder then that we find many of the distinguishing characteristics of Old Comedy in *The Taming of the Shrew*.[11] Much of its plot is dialectical rather than teleological, for the action proceeds by a sequence of encounters, or *agons*, between Petruchio and those he sees as impostors to his power. Although these contests are primarily verbal, they are often accompanied by physical violence: Petruchio wrings Grumio's ears, kicks and strikes his other servants, hurls food about his house, throws sops in the sexton's face, beats the tailor with his own yardstick, and generally manhandles Kate throughout. The looser, dialectical structure of the Old Comic plot also provides occasion for the long harangue, less suitable to New Comedy because it interrupts action. Petruchio, as we have already noted, is a great haranguer: he hardly delivers a speech which is not some kind of public performance or lecture, whether he be describing his disdain for Kate's reputation as a shrew – 'Think you a little din can daunt mine ears?' (I. ii. 200) – warning a wedding company against the dangers of stopping his way with his wife, or abusing a terrified tailor. The harangues in this play, however, do not belong only to Petruchio; Biondello before the wedding and Kate at the final marriage feast also deliver them.

Perhaps the most obvious way in which *The Taming of the Shrew* seems indebted to Old Comedy, however, is in its drive toward fantasy. Critics have long noted how the world of dream is shadowed forth by many of the play's particular qualities – physical violence which never really hurts anyone; sudden changes of dress and motivation; confusion of time sequence, names, and places; strange comings and goings; curiously repeated actions; and, finally at the end, sudden and easy satisfaction of desires. So strong, in fact, is the impression of a dream world in this play that the most interesting critical reading of it argues that Petruchio is really a wish-fulfilling self dreamed into existence by the sleeping Christopher Sly, who himself longs to be a shrew-tamer.[12] This interpretation is perhaps far-fetched (mostly because it underestimates the complexity of what Petruchio teaches and Kate learns), but it testifies to a predominant strain of fantasy in the play. Here, as in Aristophanic comedy, the hero presides at the end over a feast celebrating the victory of the impossible over the actual. Here, too, he is paid reverence, almost like a god: Kate presents her devotions to him. And then, in the final moment of the play, he is declared a miracle-worker: ' 'Tis a wonder, by your leave, she will be tamed so' (V. ii. 189).

Yet the outlines of the convention are again misleading; they would reduce the play to a mere shadow of its full-bodied form. For *The Taming of the Shrew* is really no more an Old Comedy than a New one. There is, for example, nothing in the tradition of Aristophanes to account for the Bianca plot – clearly descended from New Comedy – or for the way it is used throughout as a balance and complement to the main action.[13] More important, Petruchio's triumph is not as direct and uncomplicated as the pattern of Old Comedy suggests. He may be offered devotion like a god, but the offering, like his own earlier actions as shrew-tamer, is really a complicated kind of play that his wife has learned from him. Her speech is undoubtedly proof of her pronounced debt to him, for it takes as its model his own harangues – hyperbolic public performances depending for their effect primarily upon the spontaneous generativity of language, both in imagery and sound. Yet the very nature of Kate's performance *as* performance suggests that she is offering herself to Petruchio not as his servant, as she claims, but as his equal in a select society which includes themselves, the playwright, and perhaps a few members of his audience: those who, because they know that man is an actor, freely choose and change their roles in order to avoid the narrow, imprisoning roles society would impose on them. Petruchio, then, is not alone victorious in the final scene. Part of the victory belongs to Kate, as her exalted position as the center of attention suggests. And from a dramatic standpoint at least, it is *her* scene, dominated, and in large measure defined, by her major speech in the play.

The conventions of Old Comedy take no notice of Kate, although she demands to be noticed in this play. Again *The Taming of the Shrew* resists traditional modes of classification, and perhaps it is time to see this resistance as an essential part of Shakespeare's meaning. Like his hero and heroine, the author himself may be rebelling against form in this play. Perhaps *The Taming of the Shrew* began as an experiment against form.[14] That surely is how the Induction begins. And before it is done, it wreaks such havoc with convention that even today we cannot quite fit it to the play.

The greatest problem posed by the Induction is that it seems incomplete. Shakespeare, having introduced Sly, the Hostess, the Lord, Bartholomew Page and others, gives them some stage business and then mysteriously consigns them to oblivion, while he turns to another play altogether. But although the Induction may be incomplete, it is not incoherent, since its themes foreshadow those of the main play. Many of its concerns – uncertain and imposed identity, change of dress, violence, war between the sexes, and an insistent focus, in Anne Righter's phrase, on the idea of the play[15] – reappear in the Bianca and shrew-taming plots. Then, too, the Induction serves as a kind of dramatic tone painting which sets a mood for the work as a whole, preparing the audience for the farce to follow. Let us see how.

The Induction begins with an enormous explosion of energy. From off stage we hear sounds of a quarrel, and perhaps glass breaking, and then Sly reels across the stage in drunken flight from the enraged Hostess. He promises violence, and she no doubt inflicts it, as they argue about his bill and trade insults until she realizes she can do nothing to control the drunken rogue and runs off to fetch the law. Sly, too drunk to care about her beatings or threats, hurls a senseless challenge after her and then passes out. The brief episode is a theatrical *tour de force*, a violent shattering of stage convention.[16] For instead of traditional dramatic exposition, like a Prologue or a clear summary of problems at hand, Shakespeare gives us an explosion. Then, almost as suddenly as this episode began – and before we really know what it is about – it is over, and the stage is quiet again so that the audience can have the kind of beginning it expected in the first place: enter a lord and his servants at leisure. After disruption, a return to normality. But now the more conventional beginning confuses us, because we wonder about the one Shakespeare has apparently abandoned. Why is what was so spectacularly begun, so quickly over? When is the thirdborough going to come? Why has Shakespeare left Sly on stage? Is it so that the Lord can discover him? Why does the Lord not notice him? What will he *do* with Sly if he does see him? The Lord talks on about his hounds, and we wait impatiently for something to happen.

In the process we may also become vaguely aware of themes from the earlier episode repeated in different tones. There is talk of money and an argument which, though it is nothing like Sly's fight with the Hostess, still provokes an insult: 'Thou art a fool.' (Ind. i. 26). We hear again of 'cold' but now the reference is to a scent in the hunt. This dramatic world provides a marked contrast to the disordered one we first saw, but something of that first world lingers here still, not only in the heaped figure on the stage but also in the distant echoes of the language. Then the worlds collide. The Lord stumbles upon Sly, and like the Hostess earlier, he must decide what to do with him. She tried to beat Sly into shape and failed, leaving behind her on the stage a mass of indeterminate, subhuman form. The Lord at first tries his art at shaping this mass into a neatly ordered exemplum: 'Grim death, how foul and loathsome is thine image!' (Ind. i. 35). But soon he sees more interesting and complex possibilities for form in the shapeless mound before him – if he has but art enough. He will create Sly anew in his own image, raising him up to life as a lord:

Carry him gently to my fairest chamber
And hang it round with all my wanton pictures:
Balm his foul head in warm distilled waters
And burn sweet wood to make the lodging sweet:
Procure me music ready when he wakes,
To make a dulcet and a heavenly sound;
And if he chance to speak, be ready straight
And with a low submissive reverence
Say 'What is it your honour will command?' . . .

(Ind. i. 46–54)

Some one be ready with a costly suit
And ask him what apparel he will wear . . . (Ind. i. 59–60)

What is happening here is that the creative impulse is taking hold
of the Lord, and he is becoming a playwright, imagining the
details of scene, costume, and even dialogue. What is also
happening is that Shakespeare is disorienting his audience again.
As we expected, he has brought his Lord and Sly together so that
the action of the play can begin, but the action that then begins is
the action of imagining the beginning of a play. And that play, its
author tells us, is a 'jest.' We are now surely lost in the funhouse.
We must, however, get more lost before we can be found.
Shakespeare has barely started us on our journey through this
dramatic hall of mirrors.

The plot to make a lord of Sly is no sooner begun than it too is
interrupted. A trumpet sounds the arrival of someone of note and
the Lord, perhaps still inclining to the role of playwright,
imagines an identity and purpose for the visitor: 'Belike, some
noble gentleman that means,/Travelling some journey, to repose
him here' (Ind. i. 75–6). The hypothesis is logical enough, and
perhaps Shakespeare is just adding a naturalistic detail to his
characterization of the Lord; we all fantasize about visitors at our
doors. But this fantasy also repeats a pattern we have noted
before in the scene: it arouses the audience's expectations about
the form Shakespeare's play will take only, apparently, to
frustrate those expectations. One conventional way to begin the
action of a comedy, particularly of a Shakespearean comedy, is
with the arrival of an outsider or group of outsiders[17] – the
Syracusian Antipholus and Dromio, the Princess of France and
her ladyfriends, Don Pedro and his victorious soldiers, Viola and

Sebastian – who disrupt things as they are. For a fleeting moment Shakespeare here offers us such a beginning, and then takes it away. The imagined noble gentleman melts into thin air; the men who enter before us are merely players. Another beginning is forgotten – by everyone except Shakespeare, who eventually will make it serve double duty in his play proper:

> I am arrived for fruitful Lombardy,
> The pleasant garden of great Italy... (I. i. 3–4)

> Verona, for a while I take my leave,
> To see my friends in Padua... (I. ii. 1–2)

The players arouse our interest, not so much because of what they do – the Lord's discussion with them of a play they have acted in the past seems designed, like his earlier talk about the worth of his hounds, to allow us the freedom to pay only casual attention – but because of what they are. Everywhere in this Induction we encounter forms of play and figures of players. Sly, determined to 'let the world slide' (Ind. i. 5–6), has drunk away the workaday realm of cares and law, and now he can at least play at being someone more important than a beggarly tinker: 'the Slys are no rogues; look in the chronicles; we came in with Richard Conqueror' (Ind. i. 3–5). The Lord too avoids a world of workaday, passing his days in sport and filling his evening with 'pastime passing excellent' (Ind. i. 67). He converts his bedchamber into a kind of theater and gives his servants instructions in the art of staging a play. But hardly has he done so when he is interrupted by the fortuitous arrival of 'real' players – 'real' both by the standards of his world and the audience's, though for the audience this 'reality' is double-imaged, since the players are 'really' players playing players. In this hall of mirrors that is the Induction we find another hall of mirrors reflecting other halls of mirrors as far as we can see: Shakespeare begins a play, which is then apparently rebegun as a more conventional play, in which a Lord decides to stage a play, but he is interrupted by a group of players, who themselves come to offer service in the form of a play to this Lord, who talks with them about yet another play, which they have acted in the past but which they are not going to present this evening, when a player-lord will observe their performance of a play staged after the 'real' Lord and his servants have played out their play with the player-lord, who will sleep through the play which Shakespeare, himself playing through this mind-boggling series of false starts, will ultimately present to *his* audience!

Shakespeare's purposes here are almost as complex as his method. First, he is, like his surrogate figure the Lord, merely playing – recording for his audience the almost unbounded joy of a young man doing something whose possibilities are commensurate with his enormous energies. Second, Shakespeare's complicated play-making here is relevant to our understanding of Petruchio, whose distinguishing characteristic is his love of play and essential *joie de vivre*. This quality of life he is eventually to impart to Kate, who has to learn to direct her own enormous energies outward into varieties of spontaneous play instead of recalcitrantly forcing them into the narrowly confining roles society would impose on her. Of necessity, she will still have to play roles and to harness her volatile energies within the compass of forms, some of them tyrannically arbitrary – 'be it moon, or sun, or what you please' (IV. v. 13) – but she will have learned that since playing roles is an unavoidable consequence of the human condition, the very humanness of that condition is determined by the quality and intensity of the play, as play:

> Young budding virgin, fair and fresh and sweet,
> Whither away, or where is thy abode?
> Happy the parents of so fair a child;
> Happier the man, whom favourable stars
> Allot thee for his lovely bed-fellow! (IV. v. 37–41)

In short, what Petruchio teaches Kate is his version of a lesson of modern psychoanalysis: man feels 'only human when he plays.'[18]

Another purpose of the references to playing and play-making in the Induction is to achieve *Verfremdungseffekt*: Shakespeare unconventionally manipulates his audience's response to encourage critical awareness. So often reminded that it is watching a play, an audience cannot help wondering what the reminders are for. Why does Shakespeare keep taking us deeper into the illusive realm of plays within plays? Why does he play such havoc with our expectations about how this play will begin? Gradually we recognize that Shakespeare is wielding over us some of the same powers that the Lord wields over Sly: he is presenting us with a play which upsets our sense of the order of things. But the real purpose of suggesting such a correspondence may be to make us aware of differences. We would hope both that we are a more receptive audience than Sly[19] and that Shakespeare is doing more than merely playing a joke on us. Then, too, our consciousness of manipulated response and thwarted expectations may increase our sensitivity to such problems when they become central themes in the shrew-taming plot. There Kate's responses are at first destructively manipulated by a society which judges her – and at least has partly made her – an alien. Baptista's initial exit in I. i., when he conspicuously leaves Kate behind because he has 'more to commune with Bianca' (101) is surely an emblematic statement of Kate's exclusion from the family unit. And a similar condition of isolation from society as a whole is suggested by the way characters talk derisively about Kate in her presence, almost as if she were not there at all (see particularly I. i. 55–67). But if society isolates Kate by manipulating her, Petruchio integrates her by manipulation.

The way he manipulates her is to continually frustrate her expectations. He comes courting with praise for her beauty and mildness when everyone else has called her a plain shrew; he stands unshaken, even apparently unnoticing, against her attacks when everyone else has fled her wrath in terror; he announces he will marry her when everyone else has proclaimed her unmarriageable. But when he has won Kate's hand in this madcap manner, Petruchio has only begun to play havoc with her expectations. Greater violence is to follow – at the wedding, on the journey from home, at his country house, on the road back to Padua, and even at the final wedding feast. By then, though, Kate will have learned her lesson: that society's conventions are imprisoning not so much because they force inchoate human energies and desires into limiting forms – a necessary condition of any social intercourse – but because they can so easily *replace* those energies and desires. Forms may abide where there is no longer feeling, indeed, may even drive out feeling.

Baptista provides a clear case in point. Critics of the play have long argued about whether he really slights Kate, some attacking him because he so obviously favors Bianca, others defending him because he is patient with Kate's unreasonable temper tantrums and concerned for her happiness. In a sense both sets of critics are right, because Baptista *thinks* he loves his daughter and tries to treat her fairly. But in fact he does not. Instead of love he gives Kate only the conventional responses of a loving father. We see him first, in apparent concern for Kate, explaining that he is determined to get her a husband before he will allow Bianca to marry. However pure Baptista's motives here may be, the results are disastrous. He makes a public disgrace of Kate because she has no suitors. And then while nearly everyone in attendance makes jokes about Kate's condition, Baptista keeps returning his own attentions to his favorite daughter:

> Bianca, get you in:
> And let it not displease thee, good Bianca,
> For I will love thee ne'er the less, my girl....
>
> Go in, Bianca...
>
> Schoolmasters will I keep within my house,
> Fit to instruct her youth....
>
> For I have more to commune with Bianca. (I. i. 75–101)

Later when he talks of a possible marriage for Kate, Baptista sounds again like a loving father. When Petruchio calls for contracts to be drawn up, Baptista resists: 'Ay, when the special thing is well obtain'd,/That is, her love; for that is all in all' (II. i. 129–130). But after Petruchio has met Kate and, to all apparent circumstances, *failed* to obtain her love, Baptista still proceeds with the match, and to Gremio's joking, but probing, inquiry, 'Was ever match clapp'd up so suddenly?' (II. i. 327) he answers in a language which makes his motives plain: 'now I play a merchant's part,/And venture madly on a desperate mart' (II. i. 328–9). With no concern for Kate's feelings, he is hastily disposing of her, like faulty merchandise, to the first bidder he finds in the marketplace.

That Baptista would also marry off Bianca with similar unconcern for her feelings[20] does not alter the fact that his world is one in which conventions replace feeling. Those conventions have many forms. Love may be reduced to publicly solicitous concern or to patently possessive favoritism, as it is with Baptista for his daughters. Or it may become tantalizing flirtation, as with

Bianca; or self-generated fantasizing, as with Lucentio; or plain
and practical self-interest, as with Hortensio. It may even appear
as comically misshapen greed, as with Gremio. What matters is
not the form it has been reduced to but the act of reduction itself.
For in a world ruled, not served, by convention energies once
spontaneously felt either dissolve into cliche – Baptista talking
like a loving father about his daughters, Lucentio pining after
Bianca in the language of a Renaissance sonneteer, Hortensio
fitting his love poetry to the formula of a gamut – or lock
themselves into obsessive, repetitious behavior – Grumio's re-
current concern for food and sex, Gremio's uncontrollable
twitch toward his money bag, Kate's repeated attempts to beat
others into submission. In such a world man is threatened
ultimately by dehumanization: he can act either formulaically in
cliche or mechanically in obsession, but he cannot *act* in the true
philosophical or theatrical sense of the word because he can no
longer feel. All spontaneity, all play, disappears. 'Belike you
mean to make a puppet of me' (IV. iii. 103), Kate cries in
frustration when Petruchio will not let her have the gown the
tailor has delivered.[21] In this judgment of Petruchio's purposes
Kate is both right and wrong. Yes, Petruchio is here playing
puppet-master with Kate, making her do exactly what he wants.
But he makes a puppet of her so that she may be delivered from
her woodenness of response, from her imprisonment (to borrow
an image from *The Tempest*) in a tree: in non-human nature.
When she first meets Petruchio, Kate is a kind of puppet: hard,
grotesquely limited both in feeling and action, manipulated by a
force she cannot control. But she does not realize she is
puppet-like. In fact, she obstinately argues to the contrary:

> Why, and I trust I may go too, may I not?
> What, shall I be appointed hours; as though, belike,
> I knew not what to take, and what to leave, ha? (I. i. 102–4)

Manipulated by society, family, and her own uncontrollable
emotions, Kate cannot see what she is. Petruchio, though, makes
his manipulation of Kate obvious; he makes her *see* she has
become a puppet so that, recognizing her condition, she may
alter it, may escape from the bondage of a wooden existence
into the freedom of human form and play. That freedom is, it is
important to note, not absolute. All man's world is but a stage

and he is merely a player, an actor fleshing out a variety of roles. But compared to a puppet, he is a full and fine thing indeed. Petruchio calls Kate out of the woodenness of the puppet show into the human theater of play. And she answers, shortly, by taking command of stage center.[22]

And what Petruchio does to Kate, Shakespeare does to his audience in the Induction. He writes as if he means to make a puppet out of this audience, manipulating its responses in sudden and arbitrary ways, jerking it first one way and then another. But also like Petruchio, he calls attention to his actions by carrying them to extremes. In the process he wakens the audience to perception. He shows it that the theater it sits in, where actors play parts assigned to them, is just another form of the theater it daily lives in: 'do I dream? or have I dream'd till now?' (Ind. ii. 71). And then he invites the audience to join with him in the act of playing: its role will be, of course – audience. The role is not to be taken lightly. Mere polite attention will not serve, for that is not playing the role of audience: it is slipping woodenly into convention, which for Shakespeare is little better behavior at a play than nodding drunkenly into sleep. 'My lord, you nod; you do not mind the play' (I. i. 254–5), a servingman tells Sly, but the words are addressed also to the audience of Shakespeare's play. For if this audience does not 'mind' the play, does not bring to it all energies and faculties of mind in an effort to join with the author in *his* play of mind, then it is hardly a better audience than Sly, obliviously sleeping through a performance offered up for his delight and benefit.

An audience which was actively minding Shakespeare's play, for instance, might notice that Petruchio masters his world by playing with it. Like the Lord of the Induction, he possesses at times the vision and the powers of a playwright and director: he can both imagine a specific dramatic scene, even to particulars of dialogue and gesture:

Say that she rail; why then I'll tell her plain
She sings as sweetly as a nightingale:
Say that she frown; I'll say she looks as clear
As morning roses newly wash'd with dew ... (II. i. 171–4)

If she deny to wed, I'll crave the day
When I shall ask the banns and when be married. (II. i. 180–1)

And he can manipulate the object world so as to effect that scene – Kate enters on cue, meets Petruchio's advances with the kind of hostility he anticipates, and then finally succumbs to his unshakable assertions that he will marry her. But unlike the Lord of the Induction, Petruchio does not keep the play world he imagines and effects at a distance from him. Not to others – servants, pages, and visiting players – does he delegate responsibility of playing out his imagined dramas, for unlike the Lord, Petruchio does not see play or play-making as an essentially frivolous activity, a mere 'pastime passing excellent' (Ind. i. 67). For him play provides instead an existential address to the world. So Petruchio involves *himself* in his plays, not only by imagining their details, but also by playing out their action. He is a principal actor in, as well as a playwright and director of, his dramas.

In fact, it is Petruchio's identity as actor that an audience first notices. Hardly has he appeared on the stage before he and his servant begin to act out, with self-consciously theatrical words and blows, a game of wilful misunderstanding. And no sooner is *that* game played out than Petruchio assumes the role of a young man venturing forth into the world to win a wife and with her, a fortune. What Petruchio tells us about himself is always suspect, since he readily suits his language and his past history to the needs of the moment, but he himself later provides evidence that he is here only playing the role of a young man in search of his fortune. After all, he already *has* a fortune:

> You knew my father well, and in him me,
> Left solely heir to all his lands and goods,
> Which I have better'd rather than decreased... (II. i. 117–9)

Of course, Petruchio's original talk of fortune – 'My father dead, my fortune lives for me' (I. ii. 192) – refers to much more than money, as we shall soon see, but so energetic and apparently single-minded is his play in the role of fortune-hunter that we may forget he has set out to master the world, not merely to accumulate money, which provides only one sign of such mastery.

Another sign of this mastery is Petruchio's capacity to convert life to imagined drama and the object world to a stage on which, as principal actor, he can play out that drama to a successful conclusion. Such play engages him in a wide variety of acting roles: servant-beater, young man on the make, braggart, hard-bargaining businessman, lover, tyrant, boor, sot, near rapist, hero, animal trainer, jailer, apparent madman, and miracle-worker, to name just the most obvious ones. More important than the variety of these roles, however, is the self-assurance which Petruchio brings to them. To everything he does, to every role he plays, Petruchio brings the boundless energy of youthful self-confidence; never for a moment does he seem to doubt his capacity to master the world which is all before him. Indeed, so sure of himself is Petruchio that he converts life's challenges to something very like child's play: first he carefully limits the parameters of the object world before him; then he assimilates that delimited world, in the process reshaping it to satisfy the demands of his ego; and finally he turns this assimilated and restructured world to his purpose within the world before him. For an example of this process in its most elemental form we need only to look again at Petruchio's early commentary on his condition: 'My father dead, my fortune lives for me.' What we notice first about this sentence is the way Petruchio turns potential tragedy to a condition of hope: no Hamlet he, for the death of his father produces not isolation and debilitation but instead the promise of new life. Almost as important as the hope expressed in this speech, too, is the way it converts an experience which might be passively suffered into one which is actively manipulated. The death did not happen to *him*; he sets it off from his experience, not only by grammatically banishing it to the strictly delimited and archaic confines of the ablative absolute, but also by isolating it, in conspicuous verbal contrast, from the fortune that 'lives' for him. Finally Petruchio in this speech, as in the play in general, turns fortune to his advantage, by assimilating it ('*my* fortune') and then making it serve *him* (it lives 'for me'). We cannot be certain whether the 'fortune' he speaks of is simply the wealth he has inherited at his father's death or the wealth of experience that his father's death has freed him to encounter, but we cannot doubt Petruchio's general meaning. He will master the potential isolation and tragedy confronting him by turning death to life: his father's death means to Petruchio only that his own fortune is yet to be lived. And the first proof of the mastery he promises appears in the way he has adjusted to his father's death, verbally and emotionally controlling it – playing with it – until he has turned it to his advantage. Here in this brief comment upon the state of his fortune we see Petruchio playing his way towards ego-mastery of the world about him. We see him doing the same thing, much more obviously and spectacularly, in his dealings with Kate, who provides the most continued and stubborn resistance to the assimilative powers of his play.

Upon his entry into Kate's world, Petruchio announces himself as a player, not only by the conspicuous theatricality of his first exchange with Grumio, but also by an act of self-conscious role-playing: he assumes the role of the fairy tale hero come to free the spellbound princess from the monster. This pattern he does not make explicit, since reality is never so neatly structured as a fairy tale, and in this version of the story the spell cast over the princess has made *her* the monster. But Petruchio's behavior suggests that he sees the implicit outlines of a fairy tale in the world before him. And if he does not see these outlines, Shakespeare certainly does, for he has Petruchio present himself, both before his audience and Shakespeare's, as a questing hero – as a young man cut loose from his past but inexplicably self-assured in spite of his inexperience. The extent of his experience we cannot be sure of – his claims that he has fought in battles and made perilous journeys across stormy seas (I. ii. 201–7) may be as empty as the claims of the brave little tailor, in the story by the Brothers Grimm,[23] that he has killed 'seven at a blow' – but we never doubt Petruchio's confidence and self-reliance. He has set forth to see the world and seek his fortune, and he announces with certainty his anticipated success:

I come to wive it wealthily in Padua;
If wealthily, then happily in Padua. (I. ii. 75–6)

Here Petruchio's self-assurance and self-delight reinforce his implicit tie to the heroes of fairy tales, again for example, to the Grimms' brave little tailor:

When he left off he counted the slain [flies], and no fewer than seven lay dead before him with outstretched legs. 'What a desperate fellow I am!' said he, and was filled with admiration at his own courage. 'The whole town must know about this'; and in great haste the little tailor cut out a girdle, hemmed it, and embroidered on it in big letters, 'Seven at a blow.' 'What did I say, the town? no, the whole world shall hear of it . . .'[24]

Then, too, the world that Petruchio encounters offers obvious parallels to the realm of fairy tales. For in Shakespeare's Padua we find a father who has decreed that his beautiful young daughter cannot be married until they all have been rescued from the monster who holds them in bondage:

> Therefore this order hath Baptista ta'en,
> That none shall have access unto Bianca
> Till Katharine the curst have got a husband. (I. ii. 126–8)

And such a rescue no one in the land has the power to effect. No one, that is, until the self-assured young man arrives and undertakes the task with enormous self-confidence:

> Be she as foul as was Florentius' love,
> As old as Sibyl and as curst and shrewd
> As Socrates' Xanthippe, or a worse,
> She moves me not, or not removes, at least,
> Affection's edge in me... (I. ii. 69–73)

> He [the king] sent to the tailor and told him that, seeing what a great and warlike hero he was, he was about to make him an offer. In a certain wood of his kingdom there dwelt two giants who did much harm; by the way they robbed, murdered, burnt, and plundered everything about them; 'no one could approach them without endangering his life. But if he could overcome and kill these two giants he should have his only daughter for a wife, and half his kingdom into the bargain...' 'That's the very thing for a man like me,' thought the little tailor; 'one doesn't get the offer of a beautiful princess and half a kingdom every day.' 'Done with you,' he answered; 'I'll soon put an end to the giants.'[25]

The parallel is not, of course, exact. Petruchio does not intend to slay the monster and marry the princess. Instead he means to marry the monster and transform her to a princess, but in the process he will slay what is monstrous within Kate's psyche. He will teach her to deal with the monster of her instinctual fears and anxieties by assimilating the otherness of the world around her rather than by trying to keep that world forever at a distance. Instead of beating the world off from her by striking at people, hurling insults at them, or restricting their approaches to her with confining cords or broken lutes, Kate must learn to embrace what at first seems alien to her: the old man on the road to Padua ('Sweet Kate, embrace her for her beauty's sake.' (IV. v. 34)), her husband in front of Lucentio's house ('First kiss me, Kate . . .' (V. i. 148)), even her rebellious sister and the widow at Bianca's wedding feast ('Come, come, you froward and unable worms!/My mind hath been as big as one of yours,/My heart as great . . .' (V. ii. 169–71)). And what seems alien she can at last make particularly her own as she learns from Petruchio to master the world around her by playing with it.

That is why the outlines of a fairy tale show through the world of this play, because such tales serve Shakespeare's – and Petruchio's – purposes in at least two important ways. First, the structural correspondence between *The Taming of the Shrew* and a fairy tale suggests a thematic correspondence. In Shakespeare's Padua, as well as in the world of fairy tales, marvellous victories may be won, terrible monsters conquered, and wondrous transformations wrought – all by human ingenuity and imagination. No less than this play, a fairy tale celebrates man's capacity to master the world around him by playing with it. First, fairy tales confine the world to the formulaic limits of 'Once upon a time' and 'happily ever after.' Next, they assimilate and reshape that world so that it is free of moral ambiguity and emotional anxiety. And finally, they turn that assimilated and reshaped world to advantage in promising the victory of the apparently weak over the monstrously strong: fairy tales teach their audience to hope, to believe that the challenges of life can be mastered. Bruno Bettelheim, writing about the constructive power of fairy tales, calls upon a lifetime of experience in dealing with children to reinforce his conclusions. His interest in fairy tales, he explains, is:

a consequence of my asking myself why, in my experience, children – normal and abnormal alike, and at every level of intelligence – have found folk fairy tales more satisfying than all other children's stories. The more I tried to understand why these stories are so successful in enriching the inner life of the child, the clearer it became to me that, in a much deeper sense than any other reading material, they start where the child really is in his psychological and emotional being. They speak about his severe inner pressures in a way that the child unconsciously understands and, without belittling the serious inner struggles that growing up entails, offer examples of both temporary and permanent solutions to acute psychological difficulties.[26]

This argument, which has very direct application to Kate, provides the second reason why outlines of a fairy tale structure appear in *The Taming of the Shrew*. For the fairy tale, by playing with the child's world of apparently unmanageable psychological difficulties which it subjects to imaginative control, speaks with particular directness to Kate's emotional condition, because emotionally Kate is a child. She may be physically a young woman of marriageable age, but she is emotionally trapped in a state of arrested childhood development. One does not need the language and discoveries of modern child psychologists to see this fact, since Kate's childishness is apparent in everything she does early in the play: in her petulance, her uncontrolled wilfulness, her violent temper tantrums, her anxiety about being rejected by her father, her jealousy of her sister, her rebellion against authority and her binding egocentricity. But the language and discoveries of psychology do point the way to a more complete understanding of the emotional depths that explain dramatic surfaces, and in this case they may also help us to understand how and why it is that Petruchio can at last teach Kate to assimilate his vision and powers.

Kate's problem, which is both cause and effect of her violent behavior, is her isolation. She fears that she will be left alone, that she is incapable of being loved. Of such fears as the deepest and most destructive of man's anxieties, Bettelheim writes: 'There is no greater threat in life than that we will be left all alone. Psychoanalysis has given this – man's greatest fear – the name separation anxiety; and the younger we are, the more excruciating is our anxiety when we feel deserted, for the young child actually perishes when he is not adequately protected and taken care of.'[27] And emotionally Kate is a young child who is perishing at the beginning of this play. To her the world seems alien and distant. She is psychologically, and often physically, excluded from the family ties which bind Bianca and Baptista: Baptista obviously favors Bianca, who is his 'peat' (I. i. 78), his 'treasure' (II. i. 32); and Bianca will not confide in Kate by revealing to her the name of her favorite suitor. Indeed, so alien does the world seem to Kate that she at times seems divided even from herself, as if her own psyche were somehow 'other,' rather than self:

Hor.   ... no mates for you,
Unless you were of gentler, milder mould.
Kath. I'faith, sir, you shall never need to fear:
I wis it is not half way to her heart;
But if it were, doubt not her care should be
To comb your noddle with a three-legg'd stool ... (I. i. 59–64)

Kate's sense of otherness from the world is also suggested by her inability to assimilate it. As she does not belong to the world – excluded as she finds herself to be from the family unit and from society in general – neither can she make the world belong to her: she is apparently uneducable, for she violently resists all attempts to instruct her. Once she nearly brains Hortensio with his lute, and repeatedly she strikes out at Petruchio when, in his initial courtship of her, he tries to convince her of – to educate her about – her worth and beauty. This resistance, so apparently at odds with normal social development, the people around Kate cannot understand. They summarily judge her 'curst' and in the process only aggravate Kate's condition – by making her feel more 'other' from them, more completely alone. Their judgment also reinforces her sense of powerlessness before the world, by encouraging her to think of herself as one victimized by supernatural, incomprehensible, and irresistible powers: she is not, and cannot be, like other people, because she is 'curst.'

    Kate's response to her condition likewise works to aggravate her fears, for her way of dealing with her anxiety, as is often the case in instances of psychological disturbance, is to employ the curiously reversed logic of the psyche. Fearing aloneness above all things, she acts as if she consciously *sought* aloneness. And so her fears of separation manifest themselves as apparent fears of intrusion or assimilation: she turns away from her father and sister, rejects society, refuses education, announces herself uninterested in the good opinions of others, holds people at a distance, violently beats them away when they approach her, and in general does everything she can to discourage the formation of any close interpersonal relationships. Of this sort of violent behavior, particularly of its manifestation in the temper tantrums of children, Bettelheim writes:

> As soon as a child is able to imagine (that is, to fantasize) a favorable solution to his present predicament, temper tantrums disappear; the hope for the future makes the present difficulty no longer insufferable.

> . . . If a child is for some reason unable to imagine his future optimistically, arrest of development sets in. The extreme example of this can be found in the behavior of the child suffering from infantile autism. He does nothing or he intermittently breaks out into severe temper tantrums, but in either case he insists that nothing must be altered in his environment and the conditions of his life. All this is the consequence of his complete inability to imagine any change for the better.[28]

What Kate, then, has to learn in order to be free of the monster of fear within her is how to hope; she has to learn, in Bettelheim's language, to imagine a 'change for the better.' And such knowledge Petruchio – arriving in her world like the young hero of a fairy tale, and bearing his version of the fairy tale's message of hope – will bring to her. His way of bringing it will be dramatic, unpredictable, inventive, occasionally even cruel, since monsters must at times be cruelly treated to be conquered or tamed. But his way of bringing it will be also an important part of what he brings, since in this play, long before McLuhan, the medium is, at least partly, the message. Life *can* be mastered, Petruchio promises and shows Kate, if one develops the capacity to play with it, to embrace it rather than to push it away. His way of teaching her this lesson is to play with her, by staging dramatic scenes for her benefit and discomfort; forcing her to meet him in games of wit, physical encounter, or word-play; and challenging her to find ways of assimilating his world view so as to reshape it and make it particularly her own. But all the while that he is thus playing with Kate and so showing her by example how she too may play with him and the world, he never leaves off reminding her that she *can* master the world, that she can transform herself into a beautiful and loving princess: one who lives the joy of a close personal relationship with another human being. As Kate stubbornly attempts to push Petruchio and the world off from her, Petruchio, with the irresistible power of hope, pulls her confidently, inexorably to himself and his world of play.

Perhaps most obviously, Petruchio exercises these irresistible powers of play in the scene when he first woos Kate, which provides a paradigm for the action of the play as a whole. Kate and Petruchio first confront each other at a distance: she enters almost certainly from the back of the stage, while he, at the front, has just finished delivering in soliloquy his imagined version of the scene to come. But gradually, in spite of Kate's obvious attempts to keep Petruchio both physically and emotionally away from her, Petruchio draws her to him, until by the end of the scene he holds her in a binding grip that is partly a love embrace and partly a temporary capture. In this forced union Shakespeare, and Petruchio, present their audiences – it is not without importance that people from the world of Padua suddenly arrive to observe the loving couple – with a dramatic emblem of Petruchio's triumph: a precarious mixture of love and hate, tenderness and violence, surrender and conquest; a union that appears as yet more a product of Petruchio's imagination than a fact, but a union nevertheless – and one that, as Petruchio reminds Kate, anticipates their marriage to come.

At that marriage, though, Petruchio surprises Kate and the assembled guests with behavior that dramatically enacts Kate's deepest fear. Kate is afraid of being left alone; so Petruchio does not appear for their wedding – for a time. And then when he does appear, he shows himself apparently oblivious to the bride's feelings; he leaves her emotionally isolated and alone in embarrassment while he turns the wedding into a bizarre stage play. But here again Petruchio turns play to purpose. He stages his production so that Kate may learn that the wedding ritual, with its carefully prescribed patterns of behavior, does not make a marriage. If Kate is to be delivered from her fears of aloneness, more than surface ceremony, patterned behavior, and traditional finery of costume will be needed to effect this deliverance. She must not expect the groom, all scrubbed and shining astride a white horse, to ride up and whisk her away. Instead she must meet him, ragged and tattered by human failings, halfway. Only by mutual imaginative effort and trust can husband and wife make of a marriage the 'happily ever after' union that fairy tale endings promise marriage may be. What fairy tales promise, man and woman together *can* attain in marriage, but what they attain, they must attain *together*.

That is the lesson Petruchio carries to Kate at their wedding when he plays out a consciously exaggerated and comic version of her fear that she will be left alone at the altar of life. For through such drama he promises a kind of exorcism; he plays with potentially tragic actions until he has converted them to stage comedy. No doubt this process often recurs as a defining pattern in comedy, whose business it is first to make us look at tragic circumstances and then to deliver us fortuitously from them. But in this play a basic structural pattern of comedy is played out again and again to emphasize both the extent of Petruchio's continuing, adaptive mastery of his world and the monstrous nature of Kate's fear, which can be conquered only after repeated exorcisms.

But Petruchio does not overcome Kate's fears of intrusion and aloneness only by acting them out in self-conscious dramatic performances. Against such fears he opposes the optimistic promises of hope as well as the transforming power of play. Even when he embodies the monster of her anxieties in their most outrageous forms – as boor and cad – he continues to assure Kate that she can affect the world around her, can change things for the better: '. . . all the world,/That talk'd of her, have talk'd amiss of her . . . /For she's not froward, but modest as the dove' (II. i. 292–3, 295). This he does in part because he himself never entirely leaves off playing the role of hero for her, even when he appears also in the role of monster. At the wedding, for example, he may act as a boor, a cad, and a sot, in short, as the worst of all possible husbands. But at the end of that scene he also plays out for her his own reshaped version of the fairy tale's message of hope. He suddenly puts on the role of hero again and enacts, in parody, a rescue of the maiden in distress:

> And here she stands, touch her whoever dare;
> I'll bring mine action on the proudest he
> That stops my way in Padua. Grumio,
> Draw forth thy weapon, we are beset with thieves;
> Rescue thy mistress, if thou be a man.
> Fear not, sweet wench, they shall not touch thee, Kate:
> I'll buckler thee against a million. (III. ii. 235–41)

Behind the parody, the playfulness, of this speech, Petruchio announces his purposes to Kate. He assures her that he is willing to fight for her, to stand, as he already has, against all the world in his affirmation of what she can become. In addition, he reminds her again of what she has discovered during the wooing scene, that he possesses the power and persistence to make this stand against the world successful. And finally and most importantly, Petruchio here presents himself to Kate as her hero-rescuer, in conscious imitation – assimilated and reshaped – of the young lovers of fairy tale. After all, he *does* come to rescue her, but not in a way that she is yet prepared to understand.

A similar heroic strain appears in the monster that Petruchio embodies in the wooing scene; for although sometimes his language in this scene suggests rape, and his conduct, mad tyranny, at other times his declarations of love and descriptions of Kate's worth reflect the vision and powers of the hero, who can see what others cannot see, can do what others cannot do:

> For, by this light, whereby I see thy beauty,
> Thy beauty, that doth make me like thee well,
> Thou must be married to no man but me;
> For I am he am born to tame you, Kate,
> And bring you from a wild Kate to a Kate
> Conformable as other household Kates. (II. i. 275–80)

Here what Petruchio can see is that Kate may change; what he can do is begin to provoke that change by encouraging his 'Kate' to join with him in a heroic undertaking against the monster 'Katharine the curst.' (I. ii. 128, 129). Heroic endeavor, though, always requires dislocation from the world of previous experience, since the call to heroism by its very nature summons man out from the ordinary. Joseph Campbell, writing of the structural similarities basic to all fairy tales and myths, defines the pattern of what he calls the 'monomyth' in this way:

> The standard path of the mythological adventure of the hero is a magnification of the formula represented in the rites of passage: *separation – initiation – return*: which might be named the nuclear unit of the monomyth.
> *A hero ventures forth from the world of common day into a region of supernatural wonder: fabulous forces are there encountered and a*

> *decisive victory is won: the hero comes back from this mysterious*
> *adventure with the power to bestow boons on his fellow man.*[29]

To such an undertaking Petruchio calls Kate, first by sounding
her name, literally calling her, – 'Good morrow, Kate; for that's
your name, I hear' (II. i. 183) – and then by forcing her out from
the world of her previous experience. All that she has formerly
known he will compel her to put away, as he prepares her for the
tests to come. His way of doing this is to play out before her a
self-consciously comical version of the essential Shakespearean
tragic action – the collapse of the hero's subjective world view.[30]
Kate, wooed by Petruchio, finds her sense of self and world
altogether disrupted. Always before people have fled in terror
from her rages; Petruchio counters them with a strength that
nullifies hers. Always before people have judged her 'curst';
Petruchio proclaims her goddess-like. And always before men
have found the idea of marriage to her unimaginable; Petruchio
announces that they 'will be married o' Sunday' (II. i. 326). But
although Petruchio's carefully staged behavior in this scene
forces upon Kate the dilemma of Shakespeare's major tragic
heroes, it does not force upon her their tragedies – because
Petruchio reshapes the tragic action into a comic form. He may
render Kate powerless to effect her immediate desires in the
world at hand, all occasions seeming to inform against her as she
helplessly tries to ward off Petruchio's advances; but in the
process he offers her the hope that she may effect deeper desires in
the future, by transforming self and world. The dramatic pattern
that Petruchio appropriates for his purposes in this scene may
belong in essence to Shakespearean tragedy, but here Petruchio,
and Shakespeare, play with the actions of tragedy, converting
them to comedy. Away from the monster of death – deep
human fears fostered by separation anxiety – they tear the very
boon of life – deep human trust born of interpersonal relationships.

To find in this, perhaps the most exuberant of Shakespeare's
comedies, a skeletal structure of his tragedies is only, however,
to be dramatically reminded that comedy regularly includes
elements of the tragic vision:

> The happy ending of the fairy tale, the myth, and the divine
> comedy of the soul, is to be read, not as a contradiction, but as

a transcendence of the universal tragedy of man. The objective world remains what it was, but, because of a shift of emphasis within the subject, is beheld as though transformed.[31]

The victories attained in comedy are almost never won without being first apparently lost: madness, isolation, loneliness, self-betrayal, fear, distrust, villainy, infidelity, and even the threat of death belong almost as much to the particulars of this study as to one on the tragedies. But here, instead of proving man merely a poor player, who struts and frets his hour upon the stage of life as he unsuccessfully tries to manage the world outside himself, these threatening problems attest to man's capacity, as a successful player, to assimilate the world outside the self. Sometimes such success occurs quickly and with ease: Petruchio's insatiable appetite for play sharks up nearly everything around him. Sometimes such success occurs slowly and with the greatest of difficulty: Kate learns only very gradually to embrace the world outside her. So when the focus of the play shifts from what Petruchio teaches to what Kate learns, the violence of the action, emphasizing Kate's sense of otherness in the world separate from her, edges up against the parameters of tragedy. And for a time Petruchio seems more villain than hero. He carries Kate off to a distant, undesignated place of cold and isolation, and there he brutalizes her. Starving her, depriving her of sleep, and even tearing clothes away from her, Petruchio turns animal trainer and directs her energies to the task of taming the beast before him:

> My falcon now is sharp and passing empty;
> And till she stoop she must not be full-gorged,
> For then she never looks upon her lure.
> Another way I have to man my haggard,
> To make her come and know her keeper's call,
> That is, to watch her, as we watch these kites
> That bate and beat and will not be obedient. (IV. i. 193–9)

For Petruchio his behavior continues to be play: he still self-consciously stages dramatic performances, as his soliloquy here makes clear; and these performances, which turn the violence of Kate's earlier behavior against her – 'He kills her in her own humour.' (IV. i. 183) – teach Kate to know herself better by offering her a dramatically exaggerated picture of the monster she has been. But for Kate, and sometimes for us, Petruchio's play seems perversity, because neither Kate nor we are distanced from it as we have been in the past. In the wooing scene Petruchio's potential brutality, so obviously theatrical, did not impose pain on Kate, who met his violence with a violence of her own; so we did not feel pain either. And at the wedding and on the journey away from Padua, Petruchio's most boorishly ugly acts, his desecration of the wedding ceremony and his abandonment of Kate in the mire, occur off-stage and come to us only through the mediating narratives of Gremio and Grumio. Since they find Petruchio's behavior both wondrous and entertaining, we do too. But once Kate has been brought to Petruchio's castle of terrors, and we *see* her suffer his violence in repeated acts of brutality, we feel some of her pain. We feel it not only because we now see Petruchio's brutality directly before us, but also because Kate now seems to feel pain from the violence he inflicts: her sympathy for the suffering experienced by the servants gives evidence that she now counts herself among a community of discomforted beings. And although such a response, as a first assimilation of others' feelings, signals the beginning of her emotional and spiritual rejuvenation, it also touches the felt pain of tragedy. Kate may not feel her ties to suffering humanity so deeply or so movingly as Lear on the heath, but her 'Patience, I pray you; 'twas a fault unwilling' (IV. i. 159) shows a germ of the emotions which compel Lear's sympathy at the sorrows of poor, naked wretches.

This suffering Kate feels because Petruchio is cutting away at her defensive violence by subjecting her to a harrowing rite of passage. First he removes her from society, tearing her roughly away from all that she has known; and then after a frightening nighttime journey which suggests descent into the earth, he brings her to a place of evil enchantments. There, wielding sorcerer-like power over the object world (which he throws and kicks about at will), he imprisons her and subjects her to strange trials. For Kate, who has feared being alone, these trials are indeed most terrible: she finds herself completely isolated and powerless before the tyranny of her monster-husband. This is the world of marriage as she most feared it – isolating, entrapping, physically painful, absolutely controlled by the husband who cares only for his own satisfaction even as he talks of hers.

And so powerless is she to effect any of her desires in this world that she is deprived even of the basic necessities of life: food, sleep, and clothing. As magician-sorcerer playing much more seriously with the same manipulative powers that the Lord exercised in the Induction, Petruchio directs Kate to the dark center of her psyche and dramatizes her fears so that she may recognize them. He shows her what she has become, not only by killing her in her own humor but also by presenting her with a dramatic image of her own emotional condition: he acts out for her the drama of her true self held in bondage by her tyrannical, violent self. What is internal, in Kate's psyche and in her emotional condition, Petruchio makes external.

It is partly for this reason that Kate feels pain in these scenes, for in them Petruchio's play forces on her the beginnings of self-awareness and the painful knowledge that she has effected what she most fears. It is partly for this reason, too, that Kate's journey to, and imprisonment in, Petruchio's house suggests the fluid action of dreams – where the self is strangely powerless to repel violence; the object world of food and clothes keeps slipping into insubstantiality; persons from the outside world (Hortensio, the tailor, and the haberdasher) appear suddenly and are appropriated for particularly limited uses; and time passes illogically and indeterminately. Petruchio's play, then, summons up Kate's nightmare world and forces upon her the essentially interior journey of Campbell's monomythic hero:

> Even when the legend is of an actual historical personage, the deeds of victory are rendered, not in lifelike, but in dreamlike figurations; for the point is not that such-and-such was done on earth; the point is that, before such-and-such could be done on earth, this other, more important, primary thing had to be brought to pass within the labyrinth that we all know and visit in our dreams. The passage of the mythological hero may be overground, incidentally; fundamentally it is inward – into depths where obscure resistances are overcome, and long lost, forgotten powers are revivified, to be made available for the transfiguration of the world.[32]

That journey of emotional exploration and awakening is also, as Campbell points out, a journey of spiritual renewal; with self-knowledge comes the capacity to assimilate what is other-

than-self – at first in the simple animal act of eating, and later in
the complex human achievement of ordering the heavens and the
earth, of shaping them to one's purposes:

> Pardon, old father, my mistaking eyes,
> That have been so bedazzled with the sun
> That everything I look on seemeth green... (IV. v. 45–7)

What Kate thus experiences during her trials at Petruchio's
country house is a rite of passage which frees her from the
tyranny of her infantile self and releases her into the true
adulthood of marriage and mutuality. But before that release,
Petruchio puts her to tests both physical and spiritual so that she
may prove worthy of the vision he offers her. Not unlike the
questor for the grail she comes, after journey and prayer, to a
place of perilous trials[33] where her heroic nature is tested: there
she encounters strange and threatening voices, a magician-
sorcerer, and the ruins of failed questors who preceded her ('You
peasant swain! you whoreson malt-horse drudge!' 'Take that,
and mend the plucking off the other.' 'You whoreson villain! will
you let it fall?' (IV. i. 132, 151, 158)). Even the forces of nature, in
the form of time, are commanded to submit to the magician-
sorcerer's powers in this place of peril: 'I will not go to-day; and
ere I do,/It shall be what o'clock I say it is.' (IV. iii. 196–7).

However mad and wilful Petruchio's assertions about the time
of day here may seem to be, they have purpose. First, they
dramatically force upon Kate the fact that she must learn to
accommodate even the most apparent arbitrariness of the world
outside herself if she is ever to complete her journey towards
emotional fulfilment, towards full social and spiritual integration in 'thy father's house' (IV. iii. 185). Second, these assertions
again give dramatic emphasis to Petruchio's abiding belief in the
transfiguring power of play, to his sense that man *can* shape his
life to accord with his desires not only in its dull particulars – in
the cooking of food, the making of beds, the training of servants,
the trimming of fashions – but also in its enterprises of great
pitch and moment – in the affairs of love and time. Once again
Petruchio instructs Kate by showing her how to hope. Third,
Petruchio's assertions about time are *true* assertions – in the
world of the imagination – both because they remind us that in a
play time always submits to the controlling powers of the

playwright, and also, and more importantly, because they mark the direction of Kate's ascent from the darkness of psychic disorder back into the daylight world of social intercourse. For this reason, too, the specifics of the argument take on thematic importance. Kate claims that it is afternoon and they cannot reach Baptista's house before evening suppertime; Petruchio asserts that it is morning and they can arrive in time for the early afternoon dinner feast. Kate speaks of literal, Petruchio, of symbolic, time. By the clock it may be two p.m. in Petruchio's country house, but at this moment Petruchio does not concern himself with clock time. His interest rather is in the process of Kate's emotional rejuvenation, and in that process the time is yet morning, still at its early beginnings, with the journey toward full emotional integration yet to be made. But this journey, if opportunely undertaken now, can lead her soon to the harmonious emotional and social joy of mid-day 'feast and sport' (IV. iii. 185).

To this argument, which she does not yet really understand, Kate grudgingly submits, but even such reluctant submission gives evidence of her newly acquired ability to accept a world she formerly pushed away from her. And Petruchio insistently pushes Kate forward – 'Come on, i' God's name; once more towards our father's' (IV. v. 1) – in the direction of this acceptance; he even compels her to admit, although she does not yet consciously recognize, that she is still emotionally and psychologically more in the dark than in the light: 'Forward, I pray, since we have come so far,/ And be it moon, or sun, or what you please . . .' (IV. v. 12–13). Once she has admitted to this fact, however, Kate moves much closer to the daylight world of human social interchange. So the moon may become the sun, and Kate as well as Petruchio may begin to play with the object world before her:

> Then, God be bless'd, it is the blessed sun:
> But sun it is not, when you say it is not;
> And the moon changes even as your mind. (IV. v. 18–20)

By appropriating the image of the moon to her particular purposes here, Kate begins to follow Petruchio's lead as a player. Her first effort at play is hardly very energetic or imaginative – she uses the moon imagery in the most conventional of ways – but it provides a beginning nevertheless: she first limits the object world confronted ('when you say it is not') and then shapes that world to her very particular purposes ('And the moon changes even as your mind'). While accommodating Petruchio's vision, she playfully reaffirms her own by suggesting that he is mad – moonstruck. Then she continues the kind of play she has learned from Petruchio with new-found energy and joy: no object is too 'other' to be assimilated, transfigured, and turned to new life by her imaginative powers:

> Young budding virgin, fair and fresh and sweet,
> Whither away, or where is thy abode?
> Happy the parents of so fair a child;
> Happier the man, whom favourable stars
> Allot thee for his lovely bed-fellow! (IV. v. 37–41)

In her response to Vincentio, Kate seems to have so fully approached Petruchio's vision that she talks like him. The speech has about it the spontaneous energy and wilfully dramatic qualities of Petruchio's earlier performances: it is joyfully excessive, self-consciously rhetorical, broadly expansive – and apparently mad. Furthermore, Kate concludes this ridiculous encomium with a verbal play that Petruchio has earlier practised on her: imaginative retirement to the bed-chamber. She can now play with the idea of close interpersonal relationships, while before she could only strike out in violence against them. And since this speech is almost certainly accompanied by the physical embrace which Petruchio urges upon Kate – 'Sweet Kate, embrace her for her beauty's sake' (IV. v. 34) – Kate now takes what is 'other' into the self physically as well as emotionally: the embrace gives dramatic emphasis to the act of imaginative assimilation. And this action in turn anticipates the more important embrace which concludes the next, and last, scene, when Petruchio, acknowledging that Kate has finally become imaginatively and emotionally one with him, draws her physically into the compass of his private world: 'First kiss me, Kate...' (V. i. 148).

The final scene, highlighted by Kate's public celebration of the duties a wife owes her husband, provides a fitting conclusion to her education in a number of different ways. First, it offers dramatic fulfilment to the fairy tale whose outlines have regularly shown through Kate's story: at last the hero – here in the persons of Petruchio and Kate together – has succeeded in freeing the princess from the monster; and she appears in full regal splendor, striking all with wonder and embodying, in both her person and her behavior, the promise of new order in the kingdom:

> Marry, peace it bodes, and love and quiet life,
> And awful rule and right supremacy;
> And, to be short, what not, that's sweet and happy?
>
> (v. ii. 108–110)

Second, in its suggestion of dramatically embodied wish-fulfilment, this scene brings Kate the emotional satisfaction of effecting desires long felt but little acknowledged – to become the center of approving communal attention, to win the unqualified praise of her father, to see her sister misbehave and suffer public reprimand, and to gain a husband's admiring love. Third, and most important, it presents a revised version of Kate's original wedding celebration and so offers her the opportunity to redeem past failures by playing with them, by repeating and in the process correcting them. At her wedding Kate was torn away from family and friends before she could even begin to enjoy the post-marriage feasting, and there, too, her husband, boorishly disrupting the wedding ceremony and celebration, turned all attention away from her and toward himself, making her less an honored bride than an abused victim. Here, however, Kate is actively included in the feasting which celebrates social harmony, and here, too, her husband, capriciously interrupting the dinner feasting and fun, turns all attention temporarily away from himself and toward her, revealing her as true bride rather than as suffering victim. For in speaking of the duty that a wife owes her husband, Kate speaks also of the duty a husband owes his wife; she describes the mutual responsibility and trust necessary to any successful marriage. But that is not all she does in this scene. In addition, Kate plays both with Petruchio's publicly announced view of marriage and with her own past failures.

Some of the failures that she plays with and corrects we have already noted: she here wins her father's, and society's, public approval; she gets the better of her sister, who has always stolen loving attention and praise from her; and she makes herself the center of attention at the celebration she and Petruchio together convert to their wedding feast. But the most significant failure that she masters here is her earlier inability to understand Petruchio's vision and powers. And that failure she redeems by active assimilation. First she recapitulates its particulars while using them as examples of improper behavior in a loving wife:

> Fie, fie! unknit that threatening unkind brow,
> And dart not scornful glances from those eyes,
> To wound thy lord, thy king, thy governor:
> It blots thy beauty as frosts do bite the meads,
> Confounds thy fame as whirlwinds shake fair buds,
> And in no sense is meet or amiable.
> A woman moved is like a fountain troubled,
> Muddy, ill-seeming, thick, bereft of beauty;
> And while it is so, none so dry or thirsty
> Will deign to sip or touch one drop of it.
> Thy husband is thy lord, thy life, thy keeper . . . (v. ii. 136–46)

In her cautionary introduction here Kate shows how fully she has mastered her earlier failures, by appropriating details of the wooing scene ('threatening unkind brow'), the wedding ('confounds thy fame'), the journey ('muddy,' 'bereft of beauty'), the ordeal of the country house ('so dry or thirsty'), and her eventual acceptance of Petruchio's vision ('Thy husband is thy lord, thy life, thy keeper'). And then she playfully begins to make her own use of that vision. In celebrating the joys of marriage, she almost exactly reverses the details of her married life with Petruchio. The role of the husband, she says, is as:

> one that cares for thee,
> And for thy maintenance commits his body
> To painful labour both by sea and land,
> To watch the night in storms, the day in cold,
> Whilst thou liest warm at home, secure and safe . . .
> (v. ii. 147–51)

Here Kate paints a verbal picture of a wife's quiet, secure, domestic life in marriage to show Petruchio that though she has not herself experienced such apparent domestic tranquility, she has now achieved an emotional union with him for which the 'happily ever after' scene she describes is the traditional emblem. Whether she herself desires such a quiet life, we cannot know. What we can know, though, is that she has appropriated the details of her imprisonment in Petruchio's country house to her purposes here, by reversing them. Playing with the conventional imagery of marital bliss in a much more complex and imaginative way than she earlier played with conventional imagery associated with the moon, she shows Petruchio that he has led her to the traditional joy promised in marriage by a most unconventional means. She thus here answers his earlier play with an elaborate dramatic performance of her own, and this performance, in turning past failures to advantage, offers an example of play in a multitude of forms – as spontaneous joy, as ego-mastery, as true interpersonal exchange, as imaginative creation, and as assimilative vision. From such play Kate gains not only the pleasure of successfully meeting a potentially difficult situation, of mastering her former failures, and of manipulating the world outside the self, but also the loving and public approval of the man whose vision and powers she has assimilated: 'Why, there's a wench! Come on, and kiss me, Kate' (v. ii. 180). At last Kate and Petruchio have together achieved the fairy tale ending that he, at once embodying and exercising the transfiguring power of play, has taught her to hope for and believe in.

4 Parody and Play in *A Midsummer Night's Dream*

With *A Midsummer Night's Dream* Shakespeare shifts the focus of his attention away from the player as triumphant world-shaper – away from Petruchio who would fain be doing in his world – and towards the playwright who, though still a successful world-shaper, yet works upon that world from without rather than from within. As we watch *The Taming of the Shrew*, we wonder at the achievements of Petruchio, who can turn the apparently intransient Kate into the heroine of his self-enacted fairy tale; as we watch *A Midsummer Night's Dream*, we marvel at the accomplishments of the playwright, who can weave so many diverse strands of plot and character into the shimmering web of his dramatic fairyland. The worlds of the two plays do have much in common: physical violence that, because it seems to hurt no one, causes us laughter not pain; a general atmosphere of dream, with its confusions of time, space, and object; strange and sudden mistakings and metamorphoses; a self-assured, self-centered player cast in the role of lover but yet showing at times the chief humor of a tyrant; and warfare between man and woman at last publicly resolved. But in spite of these similarities, it is the difference between *The Taming of the Shrew* and *A Midsummer Night's Dream* that we notice: the first play belongs to its principal character; the second, to its playwright.

As it is almost impossible to talk about *The Taming of the Shrew* without focusing upon the actions of Petruchio, whose playing repeatedly and conspicuously solicits the attention of an audience, so it is just as difficult to discuss *A Midsummer Night's Dream* without concentrating on the achievements of Shakespeare, whose playwriting so dramatically calls attention to itself. No doubt this effect results partly from the fact that there *is* no principal character in *A Midsummer Night's Dream* because of the plot's multi-plex structure: no character or plot line receives enough attention to be called 'principal' – the longest part in the play, Bottom's, is hardly half the length of Petruchio's – but that fact is precisely my point. In a sense everyone in *A Midsummer Night's Dream* is a minor character, whose importance derives from the use to which he is put by the playwright; and although all characters in all plays attain to their importance in this way, we are rarely as conscious, as we are in this drama, of the playwright's part in shaping his creation.

One way to see how the playwright directs attention towards his achievement in playwriting is to look at what he does to the figure of the player in this work. For the character in *A Midsummer Night's Dream* who most resembles Petruchio, the all-conquering hero of *The Taming of the Shrew*, is Bottom, the all-confounding ass. Bottom shares with Petruchio his energy, his self-confidence, his capacity for play – for assimilating what is around him into the world of his ego. Like Petruchio, too, he plays the part of lover and tyrant, and, during the time that he retreats into an insulated world with a spellbound fairy princess (or queen) he turns temporarily into a monster. Finally, also like Petruchio, Bottom is cast in the role of hero by an audience of his peers, who recognize him as the only one among them capable of an heroic undertaking. Yet here again similarities matter principally because of what they tell us about differences. Bottom is a parody of Petruchio: he is the fairy tale hero of humble origins who never transcends those origins; he is a player with Petruchio's all-consuming appetite for assimilation but without Petruchio's capacity to turn what he assimilates to effect. As a player Bottom is a creature all of appetite. He may greedily assume the roles of tyrant, lover, lion, Thisbe, and Pyramus, but every part he plays he absorbs completely, turning them all to Bottom.

So self-absorbed is Bottom's Pyramus, for instance, that he cannot even make his audience of young lovers see the correspondence between his lamentable comedy with Thisbe at 'Ninny's' tomb and the lovers' own earlier confusion in the woods. To this self-absorption the mechanicals' wonderfully inept production of *Pyramus and Thisbe* gives clear emphasis, for one of the qualities of Quince's play which keeps it from being dramatic is that Pyramus and Thisbe rarely notice each other. They hardly communicate. Instead they speak to themselves in

declamation, even when they are nominally speaking to someone else. For this reason, Bottom the player is, as Quince claims,
though for other reasons than he knows, perfectly equipped to
play Quince's Pyramus; he is the actor as child, still incapable in
his infantile egocentricity of differentiating clearly between self
and other.

Why, however, should Shakespeare subject the figure of the
comic hero to such a deflation? It is the most striking transformation in a play distinguished by its striking transformations, for in
the way of metamorphoses, affixing an ass head on one who is
already metaphorically an ass is not nearly as surprising as
converting Petruchio to Bottom. Admittedly, that conversion is
not direct. Bottom is not immediately *recognizable* as Petruchio
transformed, for he is a Shakespearean clown, and Petruchio, a
comic hero. As a consequence, the range of their worlds, of their
talent for play, of their self-awareness, extends to different
reaches, as does their capacity to affect these worlds.[1] But calling
attention to the obvious differences between Petruchio and
Bottom merely begs the nagging question of their strange
correspondence: why should Shakespeare, who made the player
a hero and world-conqueror in *The Taming of the Shrew*, make
him an ass in *A Midsummer Night's Dream*?

The answer, I think, has to do particularly with the art of
playwriting as opposed to acting. Shakespeare may have felt a
need, after so glorifying the player, to give the playwright his
due. On stage the world often seems to submit to the powers of
the player, particularly when he is such an actor as Petruchio (or
Richard Burbage), striking all before him with wonder at his
play, turning everything about him – his body, his voice, his
movements, the people he encounters, the dramatic situation, the
things at hand – to his advantage. In the process an audience may
sometimes forget that it is the playwright's script which makes
the actor's triumph possible. The actor, in the root meaning of
the word, may be the doer, the performer who draws attention
to himself, but the playwright must first create the play if the
actor is going to have anything to do. As a demonstration of his
powers, then, Shakespeare may turn Petruchio to Bottom – to
emphasize that the play world of any drama belongs first to the
playwright, who coaxes it into being and who thus always has
the option of turning a comic hero to an ass, even if only to

remind us of his creative powers. Still, though, what matters most about characters in a play is not what formulas of dramatic convention they violate or parody, but what purpose they serve in the unique dramatic world created by the playwright; and Bottom is more *suited* to Shakespeare's purposes in this play than Petruchio, as we shall soon see. Thus by deflating the figure of the player in *A Midsummer Night's Dream* Shakespeare is not only serving notice that the playwright possesses the powers to reduce the actor to a poor player strutting and fretting upon the stage; he is also using the playwright's powers to give the player – now reduced from a figure of potency to one of parody – meaning.

That meaning derives at least in part from the fact that *A Midsummer Night's Dream* is a play notable almost as much for its parodies as for its other, more obvious metamorphoses. In addition to Bottom's deflation of Petruchio, the play also offers us: a dramatic travesty of the tragic love story of Pyramus and Thisbe, which doubles as a reductive version of the lovers' mistakings in the wood, and may even triple as a comic rendering of Shakespeare's own dramatic presentation of the story of Romeo and Juliet (if composed by then); a parody of the relationship between the surrogate playwright figure of Oberon and his incorrigible servant-actor Puck in the alliance between the inept playwright Quince and his uncontrollable principal player Bottom; a ridiculous reversal of the fairy tale situation of the princess held in bondage by the monster, in the fairy queen's rapturous capture of the ass-headed Bottom; and Bottom's ludicrously garbled version of a part of St Paul's Epistle to the Corinthians, in his soliloquy upon awaking from charmed sleep. What these parodies signal is the extent to which Shakespeare is mentally playing with the art of playwriting in this work, for a parody is a kind of intellectual play, which calls attention to the mastery of a particular constricting form by comically reshaping that form to new purposes. In order to understand how Shakespeare plays with the limitations of dramatic form in *A Midsummer Night's Dream*, it is thus necessary to see how he uses parody in that world. And since Bottom is the principal instrument of parody – and also an important indicator of meaning – in this play, he can serve as a point of departure for this discussion.

I begin near the end, with the fourth act and Bottom the player alone on a stage, with drama reduced to its elemental two boards and a passion.[2] Only here, for a moment, there is not even any passion, for the player is asleep, transported beyond the boundaries of the waking world by a magical charm. It is a charm of some considerable range and magnitude since Bottom is not the only one to have been affected by it: earlier it has struck 'more dead/Than common sleep' (IV. i. 84–5) the senses of four Athenian lovers, and long before that it has partly enthralled the faculties of the audience. So now, although they do not sleep like Bottom, they have been transported out of the ordinary and into a world elsewhere. In such a world strange and extraordinary effects are played on their senses, without even attracting notice as strange and extraordinary. There a tedious brief play some ten words long wears away the three hours between supper and bedtime; there the moon, new for Theseus' wedding, has already waxed to brightness by the time of the rustics' production that same night; and there Bottom may lie asleep in plain view of the audience without really being seen.

He has not even, like Oberon earlier, had to *ask* for a willing suspension of disbelief by announcing himself invisible. The lovers and Theseus have just played a scene all around him, and their obliviousness to his presence has conditioned the audience not to see him either. Thus when the lovers exit towards the temple, the audience confronts an empty stage. Only when Bottom fills that emptiness by stirring to life does he make the members of the audience similarly awaken from the binding spell Shakespeare has woven over them. In their theater seats many of them, like Bottom on the stage, will stir in surprise at what has just happened to them,[3] as momentarily the playwright makes them aware of his art *as* art.

This particular example of a Shakespearean *Verfremdungseffekt* does not, however, end quite here; instead it edges over into the beginning of Bottom's soliloquy. He begins: 'When my cue comes . . .' (IV. i. 204) and the audience may briefly share with the actor playing Bottom the very real knowledge that his cue has indeed come. By then, however, Bottom has already regained his footing literally and dramatically; and in his attempt to summon up first a company of lost players and then a remembrance of things past, he again magically carries the audience away from itself and into a 'most rare vision' (IV. i. 208).

Here briefly the themes and actions of the play are focused in a moment of dramatic concentration, whose importance is emphasized in a number of different ways. First, the alienation effect which accompanies Bottom's awakening, by temporarily interrupting the audience's emotional involvement in the play, encourages intellectual speculation about the meaning of the work. Second, the very episode itself is a conspicuous reflection of the action which has just preceded it, when the four sleeping lovers are found by Theseus and his party. Like Bottom, they all awake from the spell of Oberon's magic to contemplate a dream vision in which they have experienced a kind of metamorphosis and a disorienting love affair.

This correspondence is further underscored by the fact that Bottom's speech upon awakening comically combines the very different responses of Lysander and Demetrius to their experience. Lysander meets Theseus' questions with confusion and embarrassment; his speech is halting and unself-assured, marked by interruptions and qualifications. Demetrius, on the other hand, speaks like a man hypnotized, as if he were still under a charm – which, in fact, he is. As a consequence, his explanation seems poured out, more rote than felt. Unlike Demetrius and Lysander, Bottom remains incorrigible even in confusion. Combining their particularized responses into his own peculiar 'exposition of sleep' (IV. i. 42), he briefly plays both their parts, though, as always when he presents dramatic renditions, he transmutes them into parody. In his speech there is first Lysander-like confusion and then the rote facileness of a man spellbound, like Demetrius:

> Methought I was – there is no man can tell what. Methought I was, – and methought I had, – but man is but a patched fool, if he will offer to say what methought I had. The eye of man hath not heard, the ear of man hath not seen, man's hand is not able to taste, his tongue to conceive, nor his heart to report, what my dream was. (IV. i. 211–17)

A third way in which Bottom's awakening calls attention to itself as dramatically significant is purely technical, for here Shakespeare offers him a delight surpassing even those earlier proffered by the fairy queen – a stage all his own. By its very nature soliloquy serves as a focus for thematic meaning simply because it concentrates dramatic action into its barest essence as self confronting world. And in this instance the general importance of soliloquy is further intensified by the fact that Bottom has been, since his initial entrance, intent upon seizing the stage for himself.

Yet another characteristic of this interlude which makes it dramatically conspicuous is its language, not only because it comically reflects the different and noticeably limited responses of the two young noblemen to their night in the woods but also because it periodically suggests depths of emotional experience approaching the ecstatic, where dream, vision, and art are dissolved into a union that passes human understanding. There the distinctions of intellect, with its dependence on logic and on finite boundaries, are subsumed by transcendent mysteries[4] that have 'no bottom' (IV. i. 219–20).

Of course no such wild and whirling vision possesses Bottom at first; his initial response upon awakening is to ignore the episode with Titania altogether. He returns to the instant just before his metamorphosis, as if nothing had happened and he were still attendant upon the 'odious savours sweet' (III. i. 84) of Thisbe's breath: 'When my cue comes, call me, and I will answer.' But there is no cue, for all his company has fled – they must have stolen away while he slept – and he is still literally and figuratively in the woods. But then the memory of his strange metamorphosis breaks over him, in two waves. First there is the remembrance of what he has seen – 'I have had a most rare vision.' – and, shortly afterwards, the more shocking thoughts of what he has been: 'man is but an ass, if he go about to expound this dream. Methought I was – there is no man can tell what.' (IV. i. 208–212). The rest of the speech is Bottom's fumblingly comic attempt to find words and form for just what no man – except the playwright, who has already presented us with this scene – can tell.

It is therefore no surprise either that Bottom bungles the task he has set for himself or that in the process he trips over words in a characteristically Bottom-like way. What *is* surprising is the order periodically perceivable beneath the surface chaos of his malapropisms. Consider, for example, Bottom's marvelously muddled quotation from St. Paul's first Epistle to the Corinthians (2:9). Here there is a hint of vision as well as of foolishness, for Bottom is not satisfied to dismiss his experience merely as a dream. In addition, he must declare it unique and perhaps give it some meaningful form. That is why Bottom turns to St. Paul, in an attempt to find in the language of religious experience the ordering form he seeks. Religion does not, however, offer him what he wants, since it has very little to do with a dramatic world that, as early as scene one, – when Theseus describes the fate that awaits Hermia as a nun – views religious asceticism as hardly more desirable than death. Art is much more to Bottom's – and to Shakespeare's – purpose here, since at this moment the fool's desires draw attention to what the playwright has achieved: Bottom wishes to have his dream transformed into art, immortalized in a ballad that Peter Quince will write for him and that he himself will present in dramatic performance before the Duke.

Here surely Shakespeare is turning his art in upon itself. He began this interlude with a conspicuous demonstration of the playwright's problems and power – by emptying the stage of all apparent life, pausing briefly so that the audience might momentarily feel with the playwright the oppressive challenge of an empty stage, and then filling the void with Bottom's dramatic resurrection from a formless mass to a vitally formed personality. Now, at the end of this scene, he returns again to another alienation effect and calls attention to his own play as well as to Bottom's. For he too as playwright has had a most rare vision, particularized by outrageous metamorphoses and unions, not only of an ass-headed rustic and the fairy queen but also of myth and folklore, midsummer and May,[5] realism and fantasy, love and hate, drama and declamation, comedy and tragedy, to name just a few. And also like Bottom searching for a way to give lasting form to his vision, Shakespeare has turned to drama and offered his own specially titled *Dream* played before a duke at his wedding celebration.[6] Finally, Shakespeare too proffers his audience a dream that 'hath no bottom' – because as the creation of an artist's imagination it is simultaneously baseless, built on airy nothing, and unbounded, transcending the binding limits of reason and logic.

Bottom's statement, 'it shall be called Bottom's Dream, because it hath no bottom,' thus propounds a deceptively simple-seeming defense of art. At one level it calls art into doubt as illusory foolishness because it is viewed as dream – passing and insubstantial. But at another level the statement transcends the rules of logic and touches upon truth. At this level what Bottom has to say makes perfect sense; his unique experience is to be preserved as dream in its highest form – as art, vision, and perhaps revelation – because it partakes of what is infinite and eternal. Art as dream is simultaneously both illusion and revealed truth. For a moment at the end of his soliloquy Bottom's excitement about his dream presents a model, albeit simplified and parodied, of the playwright's motivations. Fleetingly we glimpse the playwright's shadow behind the fool.

The model, however, is not to be mistaken for the real thing. Bottom may have the instincts of an artist – to joy in the magic of working words, in unexampled flights of the imagination, and in the play of ego-expanding identifications – but these instincts are in no way informed by the education, discipline, and common sense that would put them to any productive use. As a result Bottom is an ass, not an artist. When he attempts to make words wield matter, that matter recalcitrantly signals its resistance to his control in malapropisms. Similarly, when he would speak with the golden tongue of wisdom, Bottom can do no better than 'gleek' upon the occasion. And, of course, he can never, like Shakespeare, find the appropriate words for the formulation of his dream; Bottom promises to 'discourse wonders' (IV. ii. 29) and delivers only an exposition on the necessity of clean linen, long nails, and sweet breath. His failures, though, call attention to Shakespeare's successes: we have already noted how Bottom parodies Shakespeare's earlier success with Petruchio; now we can see how his behavior emphasizes the playwright's achievement in this play.

Bottom would, if he could, play all the important parts in *Pyramus and Thisbe*, but Quince the playwright finally prevails against him. In *his* drama, however, Shakespeare grants Bottom a freedom denied him by Quince: in one person Bottom, inimitably, plays many people – and all to Shakespeare's purpose. For instance, in the scene of his awakening Bottom has, by comically reflecting characteristics of both the young lovers and the playwright, concentrated the audience's attention on thematic concerns in the work as a whole – on the challenges confronting the playwright and his ways of meeting them; on the relationship between dream, vision, art, and the impulses which ultimately take form in drama; and on the self-deluding rationalizations lovers find to account for the metamorphoses that passion works in them. In earlier scenes Bottom has played other parts to similar effect.

For example, when he is informed by Quince that he has been set down for Pyramus, Bottom wants to know if Pyramus is a lover or a tyrant, though he is quick to show the assembled company his facility for playing either part. In giving Bottom full rein here, Shakespeare is doing much that is obvious. He is entertaining·his audience with burlesque comedy; he is showing the very limited range of much earlier Elizabethan drama, or at least of the groundlings' understanding of that drama; and he is allowing Bottom to make explicit his natural and harmlessly realized impulses to tyrannically dominate those around him. But the thematic implications of Bottom's transportation into lover and tyrant do not end here. They also extend to other parts of the play, particularly to the first scene; there Shakespeare's audience, like Bottom's, encounters essentially two kinds of dramatic characters, lovers and tyrants.

Egeus, the old man who is determined to treat his daughter as a possession and dispose of her as he wills, is easily identifiable as a tyrant; and as Shakespeare presents him – bitter, arbitrary, irrational – he is hardly more complex than Bottom's 'Ercles.' Confronting the tyrant Egeus are the lovers Lysander and Hermia, who provide an obvious contrast to him: he is old and they are young; his speech is awkwardly prosaic, and theirs is regularly lifted by flights of poetic fantasy; he would stand upon his rights in Athenian law, and they would fly from Athens to a place where that harsh law cannot reach them. What is perhaps most interesting about these two young lovers, however, is not their contrast to Egeus but their similarity to Bottom. Like him in the 'condoling' role of Pyramus, they are consciously acting out the roles of tragic lovers. Of course their conception of love is rather more sophisticated than Bottom's; they have read more than he and so know love's language and conventions better. But ultimately their understanding of the experience of loving is every bit as narrow as his – and a good deal more dangerous, since they want to 'condole' for real, while he as Pyramus knows all the time that he is only playing.

Lysander and Hermia love by the book; they repeatedly speak in conventional images, with the full knowledge that they are employing convention. In fact they regularly refer to stories

about love in order to prove that their present experience is
genuine:

> Ay me! for aught that I could ever read,
> Could ever hear by tale or history,
> The course of true love never did run smooth... (I. i. 132–4)

The problem with taking convention as seriously as Lysander
and Hermia do here is something Bottom instinctively recognizes when he volunteers to play many parts in Quince's play: the
conventions are entrapping, because the nature of the lover's role
is already determined for him. To love by the book is ultimately
to surrender one's autonomy and to become just an actor-lover,
like Pyramus. Even worse, it is to assume a role which, if taken
seriously, leads inevitably to destruction: conventionally 'true'
love can prove its absolute truth only in the test of death. Some
impulses in the young lover's psyche thus actually *compel* him
towards self-destruction.[7]

   That is why Hermia and Lysander both exhibit what Henry
James in another context has called the 'imagination of disaster,'[8]
a positive fascination with catastrophe. When the lovers speak
alone together in this scene, and so can give free voice to their
conception of love, they fairly fill the stage with images of
destruction. In a single speech Lysander talks of war, death,
sickness, siege, shadows, collied night, the jaws of darkness, and
quick bright things come to confusion (I. i. 141–9). Such imagery suggests the language of two other young Shakespearean
lovers, Romeo and Juliet, who have a similar fascination
with disaster but who inhabit a world which tragically matches
the image of their minds with a corresponding violence. No such
violence is fortunately available to the lovers in this dramatic
work; for here potentially destructive impulses are diffused in
play – by Bottom and the rustics, by Oberon and the fairies,
and, most important, by the playwright himself, who repeatedly
encourages his audience's comic detachment by parodying his
plot and exposing the limitations of his medium. Shakespeare
does not, however, stop here; his magic must work one more
dramatic metamorphosis – so that what detaches the audience
may simultaneously engage it as well, so that his art and
medium may be parodied and exposed in all their frailty, and yet
still be believed.

His use of tyrants and lovers in the first scene is a case in point. There, working with character types so conventional that Bottom thinks they circumscribe the possibilities of all drama, Shakespeare still manages to quicken them with dramatic energies. Partly he does this by making his tyrant sound convincingly like a real old man, and partly too, by presenting lovers whose conventional woodenness is turned to particular thematic advantage: consciously chosen and carefully acted out by them, it attests to their youthfully limited understanding of love. But mostly the effect of dramatic life is achieved by the complex way in which Shakespeare both opposes and unites tyrants and lovers. Egeus, Lysander, and Hermia are not, after all, the only characters in this scene. Theseus, Hippolyta, Demetrius, and Helena – all lovers – appear there too, and in the characterization, particularly of the Duke, there is clear evidence of Shakespeare's complex thematic purpose. For Theseus who begins the scene as a lover ends it as a tyrant. That is not to say that he becomes exactly like Egeus; he remains throughout solicitous of Hippolyta and sympathetic to Hermia's plight, but he renders his judgment in support of Egeus and harsh law, and then leaves the stage with a reference to the 'business' of his coming nuptial – hardly the kind of judgment or language expected of a man whose sympathies seemed all with youth and love when he entered:

> ... O, methinks, how slow
> This old moon wanes! she lingers my desires,
> Like to a step-dame or a dowager
> Long withering out a young man's revenue. (I. i. 3–6)

What is primarily emphasized by Theseus' change of part here is an idea already implicit in Shakespeare's presentation of Lysander and Hermia – that in this dramatic world love and tyranny are forces not separate and sharply delimited but related and curiously conjoined.[9] Lysander and Hermia, loving by the book, commit themselves to a convention that, by locking them in preconceived roles, ultimately exercises over them a tyranny every bit as destructive in its potential as Egeus'; Demetrius, arbitrarily tossed from Helena to Hermia by tyrannous sexual passions, allies himself with the tyrant Egeus in an attempt to force his will upon Hermia; Helena, irrationally tyrannized by her love for Demetrius, betrays the trust of her girlhood friend and the promptings of her own best interests by telling him of the lovers' plans to flee from Athens. Then when the four lovers arrive in the woods, the sudden and arbitrary changes of passion which possess the men make love's tyranny at least for a time the dominating action in the play.

And the young lovers are not the only characters subjected to oppression by love's power. Theseus and Hippolyta, for instance, have approached love through a violence bent upon 'injuries' and domination. Their love has been first war, and Theseus has 'won' Hippolyta with his sword. Now he exercises enough oppressing power over Hippolyta to keep her strangely silent while the lovers plead for deliverance from Egeus' tyranny.[10] In the Duke's past, too, there is evidence of passions that possessed him and drove him to violence against another: he has been led through the glimmering night by Titania and has ravished Perigenia.

Even the fairy kingdom has its experiences with love turned to tyranny. Oberon, bent upon tormenting Titania for her insubordination, makes her madly dote upon the first wild creature that she sees. But Titania is not only a victim; she is also, in her own way, a tyrant. In the past she has misled Theseus; and now she refuses to allow her changeling child to make the natural exit from passiveness in the enclosed world of the mother to activeness in the exposed realm of the father.[11] Similarly, when she later dotes upon Bottom, she is still trying to enclose her lover and reduce him to a passive object for her to take pleasure upon. She surrounds him with her fairies, reduces him to inaction by ordering them to bring him everything he wants, and then ties him up in her arms:

> So doth the woodbine the sweet honeysuckle
> Gently entwist; the female ivy so
> Enrings the barky fingers of the elm. (IV. i. 45–7)

Here Bottom is, among other things, cast in the part of a mock-Oberon, dispatching his fairies on exotic errands and loving Titania. And perhaps, as Jan Kott argues, his metamorphosis into an ass suggests sexual potency.[12] But his identity in this scene is, like his identity in the play as a whole, much more infantile than sexual. In Titania's bower he is much more changeling child than fairy king. She keeps him prone and passive – noticeably changed from the restless, incorrigibly energetic Bottom of earlier, and later, scenes. Moreover, his interests in the scene are oral, not genital; he talks almost exclusively of food and then, enwrapped in the warm, enclosed world of Titania's arms, he falls asleep – less a lover than a baby at the breast. The tyrannous power of love as it is exercised by the fairy queen may be subtle and pleasurable, but its ultimate aim is still destructive: it seeks to obliterate the identity of the loved one as an other and to make him merely an object. Titania's bower is hardly different from Acrasia's.

Or, rather, it *might* be hardly different if Shakespeare the playwright did not keep us comically detached from it; Lysander and Hermia, even Pyramus and Thisbe, might be no different from Romeo and Juliet either, but they are worlds apart. The young Italian lovers inhabit the realm of tragedy, where choices, once made, are forever irretrievable; where error grows monstrously into catastrophe; and where the shaping powers of the artist are disguised as the inexorable workings of fate. In the comic world the constituent elements may be similar, but they are shaped into very different forms. Choices, once made, are never irreversible; error grows magically into wisdom; and the shaping powers of the artist are displayed as the incomparable workings of the imagination.

As a result, all finally escape the potentially tyrannous effects of love in *A Midsummer Night's Dream* – even the playwright, who, like his characters, though in a different way, must also contend with love's tyranny in this work. It imposes on him in the form of dramatic convention. For whether a dramatist works in the genre of tragedy or of comedy, the formulas of the conventional love plot constrict his freedom: he cannot think of a tragic love story that has not been thought of before, nor can he find a way to work much change upon the traditional comic plot which, as Northrop Frye has reminded us,[13] is at least as old as Greek New Comedy. This problem, too, grows even more acute if, like Shakespeare, the playwright working with a 'new' comedy has already written a substantial number of them. Shakespeare's challenge in *A Midsummer Night's Dream*, then, is to find a way of doing somehow differently what he has already done before. One way that Shakespeare meets this challenge is by parodying the very conventions that as a dramatist he must also simultaneously employ.

The most obvious source of such parody is the mechanicals' production of *Pyramus and Thisbe*, which blurs the usual distinctions between tragedy and comedy, turns the language of poetic drama to doggerel, and ineptly employs a number of well-worn plot devices that Shakespeare himself uses in the play. These include: confusion and mistaking caused by romantic self-absorption, the opposition of a wilful and arbitrary father, a secret agreement between lovers, their flight from a hostile social world, and the ultimate resolution of potential social disorder. In addition, the rustics' fumbling attempts to deal with the technical difficulties of staging their drama serve, like their dramatic production itself, to parody the technical mastery of Shakespeare's play. And finally, Quince's suggestion that his company of players hold their rehearsal in the woods because in Athens they will be 'dogged with company, and our devices known' (I. ii. 105–6) provides a parallel to the lovers' flight: both groups go to the woods in retreat from society, and once there both groups play out ridiculously comic and confusing love scenes.

This fact adds still more elaborate reticulation to the already complex network of parody in the play, because it makes of the woods a stage-within-a-stage and of the action played out there yet another play-within-a-play.[14] Hardly less than the mechanicals before the Duke, the Athenian lovers in the woods reach for passion and produce instead a comic interlude which delights their uninvolved audience, in this case Puck. And in the process the young lovers become self-parodies. This effect Shakespeare achieves principally by keeping *his* audience comically detached from his characters, by encouraging us to see Helena, Demetrius, Hermia, and Lysander as merely players acting out, unawares, another Shakespearean version of the most lamentable comedy of Pyramus and Thisbe. Here again, as in the Induction to *The Taming of the Shrew*, the playwright makes us notice his art – his playful manipulation of stage worlds – by presenting us with plays within plays. The lovers, characters in Shakespeare's play, take flight to the woods, to a sort of interior stage, set off in time and space from their everyday world. There, watched by an audience (Puck and Oberon) and subjected to the designs and magical charms of a controlling playwright figure (Oberon), they play out in dramatic confrontation scenes of love and hate, tenderness and violence, until at last they make their way successfully through the mistakings of this tangled plot and return to the world of everyday.

Like the world of the stage, too, the woods prove to be a place where everything is possible: time stands still and then jumps over a whole day; characters appear and then have only to declare themselves invisible to become so; lovers shift allegiance in a moment from one kind of loved one to another;[15] men fight with swords and yet never touch one another; all fall asleep on command; and magic is worked with the wave of a hand and murmur of verse. As the world of the woods here serves as a metaphor for the world of the stage, the action that occurs in that woods serves partly to parody, as well as to reflect, the action of the play. The lovers, so obviously manipulated by the magic of Oberon and machinations of Puck, often appear ridiculous in their mistakings, declamations, and sudden shifting of affection: 'Lord, what fools these mortals be!' (III. ii. 115). But (and here again we find the sort of self-reflexive complexity we have previously encountered in the Induction to *The Taming of the Shrew*) the action which the lovers' behavior in the woods, as a play-within-a-play, parodies is the lovers' behavior in the woods! Thus Shakespeare is here mentally and dramatically playing with his art form, creating a play which conspicuously calls attention to itself as a created play by parodying itself, not only in the details of its comic underplot but also in the action of its love plot as well.

This complex parody serves also as a dramatic declaration of Shakespeare's simultaneous bondage to, and freedom from, confining form. However much the playwright may long for a genuinely new plot or an original form, he cannot escape the constricting rules of the stage, with its preordained limits of time and space and its rigorous conventions of plot; but the stage, like any carefully delineated play world, offers within its boundaries its own sorts of freedom, if one will only improvise. Shakespeare's way of improvising in *A Midsummer Night's Dream* is to turn stage conventions against themselves, by showing us the artist manipulating his plot and characters, bringing them together in complex patterns and then parodying those patterns and the technical difficulties they are designed to overcome. By parody, then, Shakespeare plays his way to dramatic freedom: he laughs at his own past accomplishments and simultaneously affirms the preeminent importance of the playwright's powers by turning the previously world-conquering figure of the comic hero to an ass; he makes fun of the overworn conventions of plot and formal difficulties forced upon him while at the same time employing and conquering them masterfully; and he partly transcends the limits of his form by inventing a play of such structural mastery that it continually delights its audience with unlooked-for surprises.

For an example of this sort of dramatic freedom-within-form, both in parody and paradigm, we need to look again briefly at the episode of Bottom's awakening. There Shakespeare first raises his player up from a formless mass on an empty stage, an action which symbolically suggests the very act of dramatic creation itself. Then he moves Bottom, in search of his lost companions, all about the stage – again an action of symbolic suggestiveness. For Bottom running here and there and everywhere while yet never leaving the boundaries of the stage – Bottom longing to find a form to contain and an audience to applaud his 'most rare vision' – dramatically bodies forth the raw energies and imaginative excitement which the playwright must harness within the limits of his form and medium.

Perhaps nowhere in Shakespearean drama until *The Tempest* are the creative powers which contain this energy and excitement as explicitly drawn to the audience's attention as they are in *A Midsummer Night's Dream*. [16] And in *The Tempest* there is a kind of weariness, even if tempered by satisfaction, which finds no expression in this play. For *A Midsummer Night's Dream* is obviously the work of a young playwright exulting in the discovery that there may be 'no bottom' to his powers, even if there are limitations to the art form with which he works. Repeatedly, his delight in what he is doing – like Bottom's as he seizes upon the irresistible dramatic possibilities offered by the roles of lover, tyrant, Thisbe, and lion – erupts in dazzling displays of theatrical pyrotechnics. His very choice of subject, in which three or four radically different plots and groups of characters are developed and interwoven, is itself a thing of wonder. So is his manipulation of the lovers in the woods, where dramatically complicated problems of emotional and physical realignment are handled with dismaying ease. And so, too, is the spectrum covered by his poetic faculties, which range effortlessly from the lurching speech of Egeus to the lyrical protestations of the young lovers, from the swift and skipping rhymes of Puck to the gorgeous and exotic-sounding verses of Titania, from the easy naturalness of the rustics' dialogue to the ridiculous artificiality of their dramatic production.

Another indication of Shakespeare's self-reflexive interest in his own dramatic art is his use of surrogate playwright figures in the play. Admittedly, the presence of such figures may have much to do with the themes of love and tyranny: Lysander and Hermia trying to shape their lives into a tragic work of art, and Egeus staging his own particular play before Theseus in the first scene are hardly to be taken seriously as prototypes of the artist. The same cannot, however, be said of Quince and Oberon, for both of these characters, in different ways and in different worlds, experiment with the artist's power of invention. Quince writes and stages a play; Oberon conceives and directs two very different romantic comedies in the woods. Both, too, experience the artist's magical powers of resolution. Quince writes a prologue to resolve all the thorny problems associated with dramatic representation; Oberon dispels the young lovers' dilemma by removing the charm from Lysander's eyes, and he does the same for Titania. Moreover, in their roles as artists both Quince and Oberon are shadowed by characters who present creative energies in more primitive forms. Puck, delighting in practical jokes and in his own physical and emotional agility, surely represents instincts for play that serve the artist but sometimes run out of control. In a similar way, as we have already noted, Bottom embodies diffusive impulses for imaginative transportation which the artist must finally infuse into a local habitation and a name.

Unlike Oberon, however, Quince lacks the power to direct such impulses to satisfactory ends, either in his play or in the world outside his play, for he cannot find a way to keep Bottom and the energies he represents from disrupting his work. At the mechanicals' organizational meeting Bottom subverts Quince's attempt to assign parts by constantly interrupting him, either to offer advice or to demonstrate his natural talents for every role in *Pyramus and Thisbe*. Then later at the rehearsal Bottom's sudden transformation to an ass drives the others in disordered flight from the woods. And finally during the actual performance before Duke Theseus Bottom's personality overwhelms the character of Pyramus and so contributes to the play's failure to achieve any semblance of dramatic illusion. Quince's unsuccessful venture into the vagaries of play writing and producing thus gives comic proof of the obvious fact that a dramatist cannot succeed on impulse and good intention alone. He must have in addition that rare capacity to shape his material to the rigorous and variegated demands of his medium; he must be able to manipulate plot, character, language, properties, and dramatic conventions in order to establish between audience and actors a temporary community of understanding about the artistic world they all, with various forms of imaginative effort, help to bring into being.

The metaphor Shakespeare employs here – and in a number of other works – for the kind of play-making skill demanded of the successful dramatist is magic, which is closely tied to drama in significant ways. Both drama and magic, for example, offer more-than-human control of a particular, predesignated space which at the conclusion of the action is returned to the world of commonplace affairs; both involve uncommon manipulations of materials that set aside the usual laws governing the behavior of matter in space and time; and both depend for their effect partly on repeated, almost ritualistic actions. But what magic and drama have most obviously in common, and what is perhaps most notable about them, is their essential concern with changing things of this world into objects which satisfy desires. The magician, whether he works with cheap trickery, turning red handkerchiefs into blue ones, or with the very power of the heavens, turning a circle into sacred space, metamorphoses things. So does the dramatist, whose task it is to convert a stage into a world, by turning actors into people, language into action, and art into life. And of the dramatist's abiding concern with metamorphosis Shakespeare was more than usually aware.

Repeatedly in his plays he returned to themes and images of change,[17] finding in the subject almost endless dramatic possibilities – Antipholus and Dromio of Syracuse changed into Antipholus and Dromio of Ephesus, Christopher Sly metamorphosed into a lord, Bottom transported into an ass, Margaret changed into Hero and Hero into a soiled adulteress, Rosalind metamorphosed into Ganymede and Ganymede into Rosalind, Viola changed into Cesario and Cesario into Sebastian. Such a list, based on only a few of the comedies, is barely a beginning, but the list does give evidence of Shakespeare's self-conscious manipulation of the theme of metamorphosis, which is, of course, a dominant concern in *A Midsummer Night's Dream*. And from metamorphosis it is but small way to magic. Antipholus and Dromio think that the city of Ephesus is full of dark-working sorcerers, Kate's ultimate transformation to a loving wife is a 'wonder' to those assembled for Bianca's wedding feast, Bottom becomes the victim of Puck's supernatural trickery, and Hero is restored to Claudio from apparent death. All this is to say nothing of the characters in Shakespearean comedy who in one way or another demonstrate magical powers – Dr. Pinch, Berowne, Petruchio and his ectype the Lord, Portia, Rosalind, Puck and Oberon.

The magic these characters wield is often associated with the playwright's powers, and never more conspicuously than with Oberon. Like Shakespeare Oberon exercises his magic within a carefully delimited world of time and space, in this case in the woods outside Athens at night. It is true that Oberon once claims his powers do not dissolve with the onset of day (III. ii. 388–93) – perhaps because the magic a playwright exercises may, like Oberon's on Demetrius, sometimes imaginatively accompany an audience back into the world of everyday – and he extends his blessing to the company assembled for Theseus' wedding celebration. But the magic spells that he weaves, on Titania, on Demetrius, and (through his agent Puck) on Lysander, are administered within the fairy kingdom of the woods. And the woods outside Athens, like the Forest of Arden later, serve as a metaphor for the play world controlled by the dramatist's magic: 'This green plot shall be our stage, this hawthorn-brake our tiring-house...' (III. i. 3–4). To be sure, Oberon's powers are not the exact equivalent of the playwright's. Although he may, like Shakespeare, eventually effect a happy ending to the lovers' trials in the woods, he cannot anticipate the particulars of their further confusions. Nor apparently can he imagine the way in which Bottom will be drawn into Puck's, and Shakespeare's, plot. That narrative he has to learn of by report; he cannot bring it to imaginative, and dramatic, life himself – as he can, for instance, the story of how love-in-idleness came to have magical powers (II. i. 148–72), or the description of Titania's guarded bower of rest (II. i. 248–56), or the happy endings awaiting the quarreling lovers (III. ii. 354–73).

Oberon, then, shares with Shakespeare a number of important characteristics as a play-maker; and these correspondences call attention to Shakespeare's art: his primary focus of dramatic interest is now not the figure of the actor who, like Petruchio, shapes his world by actively playing with it, but rather the figure of the playwright, whose control of his world is less direct, as much a result of intellectual as of physical play. For Oberon, like Shakespeare, remains often physically detached from the results of his magic. Much of that magic, after all, is accomplished indirectly through his agent Puck, and Oberon himself often serves as audience to, rather than as actor in, his play: 'I am invisible;/And I will overhear their conference' (II. i. 186–7). He is not, of course, always content to be primarily an observer of action. Like Petruchio, he does declare his love to a kind of princess – in fact, a queen – only to be summarily rejected. Then in order to establish the loving union he desires with her, he places her temporarily under his bondage and subjects her to the powers of a monster, until he at last brings her to understand that her previous resistance to him is in error, and they are united in a celebration of marital harmony near the end. But Oberon's means of success are radically different from Petruchio's;[18] he accomplishes by magic what Petruchio achieves by actively playing with the particulars of his world. This is because in *A Midsummer Night's Dream* Shakespeare embodies his own magical, dramatic powers in a surrogate playwright figure, whose powers within his insulated world resemble – though they do not match – Shakespeare's.

There is at least one other reason, though, why surrogate playwright figures appear with such frequency in *A Midsummer Night's Dream* – because characters in this world regularly seek to insulate themselves from the unpredictable welter of reality by confining it within oversimplified, 'pat' (III. i. 2) forms; they would reduce the complexity of life to some simplistic formula, for which the play script, since it controls reality – actors, props, stage situations – by letting in only what the actor and his play can use to advantage,[19] is the emblem in this work. In a sense, then, the characters in this play all aspire to the playwright's power – they wish to create a script which perfectly controls reality – without putting on his knowledge – that such a script is the product not so much of simplified exclusion as of complicated inclusion. As characters in this play bumble through the experience of trying to keep contingencies out of the scripts they would compose to order their worlds, Shakespeare himself makes a success of his play by including in its script not only contingencies but also apparent impossibilities, like the union of Bottom with Titania. Everywhere we look in *A Midsummer Night's Dream* we find characters parroting formulas, murmuring incantations, trying to prepare the perfect play script, or seeking to insulate themselves from outside disruptions, but always life – and Shakespeare's drama – complicates what they seek to simplify. Again the first scene provides a useful example of this effect.

Theseus, at last having won Hippolyta, now thinks of nothing but his imminent marriage to her; and in an attempt to put away the cares of rule and close out all other concerns of state except his wedding, he orders Philostate to 'Stir up the Athenian youth to merriments...' (I. i. 12). For the next four days Theseus would have the world of Athens reflect his joy; he would insulate his kingdom against all show of sorrow ('The pale companion is not for our pomp' [15]) and live in a realm of revelry. But powerful Duke though he is, he cannot make his world as insulated as he would wish; he cannot close out all the problems of state which impose themselves upon a ruler's attention. No sooner has he declared that the time shall be given over to celebration than Egeus enters with complaint against his daughter Hermia. Like the young King of Navarre, whose similar attempt to make a beginning of his play by insulating himself from royal responsibility is cut off by the disrupting appearance of Don Armado with Costard, Theseus discovers that matters of state cannot be dispatched merely by decree at the convenience of the ruler: his world refuses to fit its action to the neatness of the script he would compose for it, for the Athenian youth dragged in Egeus' wake are hardly stirred up to merriments. They come instead spoiling for a fight – against parent, against law, even against one another. And yet what disrupts the tidy order of Theseus' play script as he would have it Shakespeare readily uses to *his* script's purposes, not only because this action puts his play into motion but also because, in the context of Shakespeare's drama, the Athenian youth who enter *are* stirred to merriment: their subsequent arguments and mistakings in this play will contribute to Shakespeare's comic action, to the merriment of this work. So although Theseus cannot see the entry of the young lovers as anything but a disruption of his plans, we can recognize it as the beginning of a conventional comic plot and so as Shakespeare's answer to Theseus' call for celebration. In a way, then, the comedy played out by the Athenian lovers serves as another kind of play-within-a-play, not only because it occurs mostly within the insulated world of the woods, but also because it presents Shakespeare's dramatic reply to Theseus' command for celebration.

Theseus, however, is not the only character in this scene who wants to confine the complexity of human action within the orderliness of an oversimplified script. Egeus, too, would tidy up life's contingencies, though his impulses are for enforced repression, not celebration. He would bend his daughter to his will and to the rigorous strictures of Athenian law:

> As she is mine, I may dispose of her:
> Which shall be either to this gentlemen
> Or to her death, according to our law
> Immediately provided in that case. (I. i. 42–5)

The script he would write for life excludes all possibility of human sympathy, and he calls upon the written word of an arbitrarily narrow law – another sort of script – to set right the disorder of his daughter's emotions; she must obey him or die. This script he would compose for Hermia's life is not only repressively constrictive; it is also essentially undramatic, since it offers characters no possibility of human exchange. Because it allows for no delay, no compromise, no qualification, no emotion but anger, it is a script more suited to the absolute laws of mathematics than to the contingencies of drama, and in order to make dramatic use of it, Shakespeare must quickly subject it to alteration. Theseus, and Shakespeare, introduce into it a qualification – Hermia may choose a nunnery rather than death – and the element of time to allow dramatic situations to evolve – she has four days to decide. Thus do they provide for the possibility of dramatic action, and for its result as Shakespeare's play.

The young lovers, we have earlier noted, also engage in an act of oversimple scriptwriting in this scene: they seem subconsciously attracted to the neatness of tragic love stories, as if they could prove the purity of their love only by dying for it; and when they are left alone, they spend time reducing feeling to formula:

> *Lys.* Ay me! for aught that I could ever read,
> Could ever hear by tale or history,
> The course of true love never did run smooth;
> But, either it was different in blood, –
> *Her.* O cross! too high to be enthrall'd to low.
> *Lys.* Or else misgraffed in respect of years, –
> *Her.* O spite! too old to be engaged to young.
> *Lys.* Or else it stood upon the choice of friends, –
> *Her.* O hell! to choose love by another's eyes. (I. i. 132–40)

But unlike the lovers and the rest of the scriptmakers in this scene, Shakespeare is not attracted by oversimplification. He sees that tragic love often results from uncertainty and distrust; young lovers may seek death in order to secure forever a relationship they instinctively fear will not only change but dissolve with time. Hermia and Lysander swear such solemn, self-important vows to one another partly because they subconsciously doubt one another, as their periodic interjections of uncertainty make clear. And this doubt, this evanescent quality of young love – as brief as lightning in the collied night – Shakespeare turns to comic purpose. As he converts potential tragedy to comedy in his creation of the mechanicals' inept production of *Pyramus and Thisbe*, so he achieves much the same effect by turning the lovers' potentially tragic experience, and subconscious distrust, to comic action. Instead of dying to prove the permanence of a love they actually fear may pass away, Shakespeare's young (male) lovers display sudden and ludicrous changes of affection – an action which gives comic expression to the same subconscious uncertainty that, in another context, produces the extremist, tragic behavior of Pyramus and Thisbe or of Romeo and Juliet.

Finally the rejected Helena, too, would simplify the complexity of experience in this scene. She would compose a script for her life in self-consciously poetic verse, which serves more to make a dramatic show of her emotions than to express them with genuine feeling. In a somewhat different way than Hermia and Lysander, she imagines herself a young lover in the romance tradition: she speaks some of the most self-consciously poetic

verse in all of Shakespearean drama. Her first speech, for
example, is almost impossibly difficult for an actress to play,
because it is so obviously artificial and composed – as if Helena
had been waiting in the wings, preparing the speech before her
entrance. It sounds like what Helena thinks a lover in a poetic
drama ought to sound like. With its accented rhyme, strained
metaphor, forced exclamations, and generally self-consciously
rhetorical composition, the speech in fact sounds very like an
educated girl's version of Quince's Thisbe:

> Call you me fair? that fair again unsay.
> Demetrius loves your fair: O happy fair!
> Your eyes are lode-stars; and your tongue's sweet air
> More tuneable than lark to shepherd's ear,
> When wheat is green, when hawthorn buds appear.
> Sickness is catching: O, were favour so,
> Yours would I catch, fair Hermia, ere I go . . . (I. i. 181–7)

This is hardly natural sounding talk, and neither Shakespeare nor
Helena intends it to be. She reaches self-consciously for poetic
effect, while he shows her turning feeling to formula, forcing
complex emotions down beneath the level of consciousness,
where they may work disruptively.

This pattern in Helena's behavior Shakespeare emphasizes
even more clearly in her soliloquy which ends the scene. For in
this speech Helena depends so heavily on traditional poetic
metaphor that we cannot always be certain of what she is saying,
and we doubt if *she* knows either. For instance, Helena seems
confused about whether or not to value love – because she is
pulled in two different emotional directions by it – and she
mixes traditional poetic formulations of love's effect, one
essentially positive, the other negative:

> Things base and vile, holding no quantity,
> Love can transpose to form and dignity:
> Love looks not with the eyes, but with the mind;
> And therefore is wing'd Cupid painted blind . . . (232–235)

Yet it is impossible to tell if Helena knows that her evaluation of
love's worth here is inconsistent. Does she understand that love

works self-contradictory effects on her emotions, or is she here merely throwing traditional poetic formulas together to insulate herself from these self-contradictory emotions? This problem becomes even more acute at the conclusion of the soliloquy when Helena decides to tell Demetrius of Hermia's flight to the woods. Why she decides to tell him this information, she does not really make clear, because she again experiences conflicting impulses. She does it, she says, to 'have thanks' (249) and 'to enrich my pain' (250), reasons which hardly seem to justify the rashness of her action. For it is distinctly to Helena's advantage *not* to convey this information to Demetrius, since if Hermia and Lysander escape together, Demetrius will lose Hermia forever and so have reason to turn his attentions again to Helena. Is Helena, then, so helplessly in love with Demetrius that she cannot see her way to her own good? Does she find brief 'thanks' now worth the risk of losing him irretrievably in the future? Or does the key to Helena's behavior lie in that nearly oxymoronic phrase, 'enrich my pain'? Is she attracted to Demetrius principally because she is instinctively driven by self-destructive tendencies that his harsh treatment of her may satisfy?:

> I am your spaniel; and, Demetrius,
> The more you beat me, I will fawn on you:
> Use me but as your spaniel, spurn me, strike me,
> Neglect me, lose me . . . (II. i. 203–6)

This question Helena never really confronts, and Shakespeare does not choose to answer, because instead of driving Helena to the self-punishing ruin she apparently seeks, he converts her potentially tragic experience to comedy. Subconsciously seeking pain, or at least acting irrationally under love's influence, Helena buries her complex emotions beneath oversimplified poetic formulations. She thus has much in common with Quince's Thisbe, and meets much the same sort of reception from her off-stage audience: detached from her potentially tragic situation, that audience sees in her mistakings and emotings only the laughable confusions of comedy. The script of the play Shakespeare writes her into is fuller and more complex than the overly poeticized and simplified drama she would compose for herself.

The tendency for characters to impose an oversimplifying dramatic script upon the complexity of human experience appears in a variety of forms throughout *A Midsummer Night's Dream*. Most obviously, the mechanicals work to create a play script that will hold at bay all contingencies from outside the boundaries of their created play world: the lion must not frighten the ladies, moonshine must come in at a chamber window or enter as a character, and wall must present a chink for Pyramus and Thisbe to talk through. But although the rustics are most clearly involved in insulating their play world against unwanted complexity, almost every other character engages at least once in a similar act of simplistic playwriting, by trying to keep the complications of life out of an imaginatively constructed and delineated world. Titania's fairies sing her to sleep with promises of a rest uninterrupted by wicked spells or vile creatures, but their incantatory magic fails to keep either Oberon's love-juice or Bottom's ass head away from the fairy queen. Philostrate tries to insulate Theseus from the ineptness of the mechanicals' play by discouraging him from choosing it, but he fails either to convince Theseus of his opinion or to anticipate how the unintended comedy of this production is suited to Theseus' desires at the moment. Theseus passes simplistic judgments against the poet (lumping him with the lover and the lunatic) and players (judging the best of their kind no more than shadows) without ever recognizing that the poet, like the lunatic and the lover, may attain occasionally to the ecstasy of visionary experience. Nor can he realize, more importantly, that for all his deprecation of players as shadows, he is himself such a shadow, fleshed out to substance by poet and player, and watched with amused detachment by a group of spectators, who, if they are no better an audience than he, may choose to judge him as insignificant as he judges Pyramus and Thisbe. Finally, Oberon, who comes closest to wielding the playwright's powers in this work, since he does eventually shape a multifaceted play to his desires in the woods, cannot always keep the complexity of his insulated fairy kingdom under perfect control: Titania for a time keeps him out of her bed, and Puck lays the magic love juice on the eyes of the wrong Athenian lover. So even when *A Midsummer Night's Dream* gives us a playmaker as successful as Oberon, we still feel the greater range and amplitude of Shakespeare's success, since he can shape to the structures and purposes of *his* play all the complexity that confounds the other playwright figures. As a shaper of dramatic comedy, then, Shakespeare reaches the height of his powers in *A Midsummer Night's Dream*, for in spite of their obvious greatness – in offering fuller characterization, greater poetic sophistication, and more complex dramatic worlds – none of the mature comedies manages the dramatic medium as spectacularly as *A Midsummer Night's Dream*. None so obviously affirms, demonstrates, and celebrates the dramatist's play-making powers as this, Shakespeare's most exuberantly self-reflexive comedy of play.

5 The Evidence of Things not Seen: Making Believe and the Self-defensive Play of *Much Ado About Nothing*

What we notice first about *Much Ado About Nothing*, if we come to it by way of *The Taming of the Shrew* and *A Midsummer Night's Dream*, is a qualified sense of the power of play and, perhaps, of the possibilities of the dramatic medium itself. After the all-assimilating play of Petruchio and the theatrical pyrotechnics of *A Midsummer Night's Dream*, Shakespeare here turns away from the dramatic celebration of his play-making powers. That is not to say that *Much Ado About Nothing* lacks dramatic energy – since Beatrice, Benedick, and Dogberry vitalize every scene in which they appear – or that it fails either imaginatively or theatrically – since most Shakespearean critics include it among the 'great' comedies and since it has enjoyed an uninterrupted history of success on the stage. It is only to say that the tone of the play differs from that of its predecessors in this study. That tone is darker, no longer reflecting the delight of a dramatist freely playing with the possibilities of his medium. In the structure of *Much Ado About Nothing*, for example, we find less of the exuberant dramatic inventiveness characteristic of the four earlier comedies and more of the mature dramatic complexity characteristic of the later ones. Here we see no outlandish and miraculous collision of duplicate sets of twins with the same names, no enlarged play-pen world insulating its inhabitants in a kind of moratorium from all sorrows and responsibilities except those of adolescent love, no fairy tale hero come to rescue the princess from the monster, and no beneficent King of the Fairies at last making all well between lovers by selectively touching them with magical love juice. Instead we encounter a set of lovers who seem genuinely human – complex, passionate, proud, vain, intelligent, self-doubting, misguided, frustrated, mistaking, self-defensive, foolish, and loving. We encounter as well a world which, like our own, sometimes will not submit to absolutist interpretation. For much of what happens in this play resists certain explanation.

Most obviously, we cannot determine the extent of Margaret's involvement in Borachio's plot. It hardly seems possible she could have dressed as Hero and played a love scene with Borachio without wondering about the purpose of such mischief. Nor can we explain her absence from the wedding and her subsequent silence when Hero's death is announced unless we think of her as somehow knowledgeable about the plot. After all, only Borachio testifies to her innocence, and he may be protecting her. Certainly criticism of the play has been protective of her. Almost unanimously critics believe Borachio and dismiss the question of Margaret's guilt as irrelevant: Shakespeare was not interested here in consistency of character,[1] only in dramatic convenience; so he sometimes presents Margaret as a character and sometimes presents her as a prop, dressed as he chooses and moved about at will. As the sensible modern critic does not inquire after the girlhood of Shakespeare's heroines or the number of Lady Macbeth's children, neither does he ask for dramatic consistency from a minor character – and dramatic convenience – like Margaret. At least probably he does not ask for dramatic consistency, but not certainly. For much in Margaret's behavior has very direct relevance to thematic concerns in the play as a whole.

For example, the fact that our knowledge of Margaret's innocence depends exclusively on the testimony of a single person, and he a villain, may not be altogether irrelevant in a play whose principal action has to do with false testimony. Neither perhaps should we altogether ignore the fact that the characters at the end of *Much Ado About Nothing* show a decided tendency to fix the blame almost entirely in a single source – Don John – as if human suffering were caused exclusively by some locatable evil-doer who can be identified and rooted out of society. Such an attitude conspicuously ignores the other human weaknesses which variously contribute to this suffering – Claudio's lack of faith and resulting desire for cruel revenge, Don Pedro's quickly wounded sense of pride, Leonato's willingness to believe slander about his daughter, Dogberry's inability to speak plainly and clearly, Beatrice's failure to notice that she can disprove Don John's charge of past promiscuity, and even Hero's confusion and passivity. Perhaps Shakespeare's conspicuously casual dismissal of the question of Margaret's guilt is designed to keep the audience from making the same mistake that the characters make when they at last judge Don John 'the author of all' (v. ii. 100–1) this confusion.

Also significant is the fact that Margaret's action of producing confusion and misunderstanding by hiding her true identity behind a false surface dramatically embodies a gesture repeated again and again in the world of this play, where a fondness for deception and disguise so often promotes misunderstanding. And though regularly practised by the evil-doers – who eavesdrop on others behind the cover of an arras, who stir up dissension among friends under the guise of solicitous concern for proper social behavior, and who slander Hero while pretending to honor the interests of Don Pedro and Claudio – such a fondness for deception and disguise is not limited to the evil-doers alone. In fact, almost all of the characters in the play show an unusual propensity for deception: Beatrice and Benedick hide their love for one another behind their merry war of insults; Don Pedro appears in a masquer's disguise to court Hero; Claudio, who once poses as Benedick when Don John addresses him as such, later pretends to the role of groom when he arrives at church intent upon publicly shaming his bride-to-be; Leonato first announces his daughter's death and then rearranges her marriage – as his fictitious niece – to Claudio; Hero appears masked, as Antonio's daughter, for a second marriage to Claudio; even the Friar dreams up a deceptive plan to change Claudio's anger to remorse. The problems associated with Margaret's strange behavior in *Much Ado About Nothing*, then, direct attention to important thematic concerns in the play as a whole – to the characters', and the audience's, dependence on what may be false testimony; to the characters' oversimplifying tendency to ignore their own contributions to the sufferings they experience or inflict on others; and to a general fascination with, and predisposition for, deception in the world of this play. Such concerns almost certainly attach themselves to Margaret's conduct by accident; she is simply a minor character, inconsistently presented. But this minor example of confusing – and perhaps uninterpretable – behavior does direct attention to major instances of confusing behavior at the very center of this work. And in turn this confusion suggests the complexity of motive and action we associate with real human beings, and makes the world of this play the most realistic so far encountered in the comedies. *Much Ado About Nothing* moves away from miracle, moratorium, fairy tale, and magic towards more realistic human feeling, frailty, misunderstanding, and mistake. That is why we find at its core questions so complex that they cannot be certainly resolved – because they suggest the inextricably tangled motives of real human action.

Consider, for instance, the problems posed by Don Pedro's proposal to Beatrice. Unlike the question of Margaret's apparent inconsistency of character, these problems cannot be dismissed as the result merely of dramatic convenience or carelessness. In *Much Ado About Nothing* Shakespeare may not have concerned himself with the small matter of consistent behavior from a minor character, but he cannot very well have played fast and loose with a moment of major thematic importance in the play. At issue in Don Pedro's proposal is nothing less than the essential nature of both Beatrice's character and the world of *Much Ado About Nothing*, and yet it is impossible to determine for certain what happens in this scene. To begin with the most basic, and apparently simplest, question: Is Don Pedro's proposal of marriage genuine? Is he in love with Beatrice? To be sure, princes in Shakespearean drama do not generally ask young ladies to marry them without meaning what they say. But the circumstances of this proposal hardly suggest that it is offered in earnest. Until this moment in the play Don Pedro has shown no evidence of love interest in Beatrice; so his offer seems to come, emotionally, out of nowhere. It is true that an actor on a stage *could* convey such interest merely by the way he looked at Beatrice and spoke to her, but almost nothing in the text before, or after, this scene suggests this possibility.

Three other things about the circumstances of Don Pedro's proposal, besides its suddenness, also call its genuineness into doubt. First, its public nature. The offer, made in the presence of Benedick, Claudio, Hero, and Leonato, hardly suggests the intimacy of a proposal motivated by love, which seems the only possible reason why Don Pedro should want to marry Beatrice, since she is conspicuously not his social equal: no one in the play is. Second, the proposal seems to come as a direct response to Beatrice's half-jesting, half-serious complaint that she may 'sit in a corner and cry heigh-ho for a husband!' (II. i. 331–2). For that reason Don Pedro's offer may be meant merely as a kind of compliment, as a polite gesture designed to remind Beatrice and the people about her that she is here underestimating her value: she does not really need to worry about becoming an old maid. In this case, the proposal is to be taken no more seriously than the rest of the verbal banter that is so often characteristic of conversation in Messina. Third, and most importantly, no one else in the play seems to take Don Pedro's offer seriously, for no one speaks of it afterwards, and surely Beatrice's refusal of marriage with a prince would provoke wonder and discussion among her friends and acquaintances. But in spite of all this evidence to the contrary, we cannot be *sure* that the Prince's offer is not genuine: he does, after all, propose to Beatrice, no matter how curious the circumstances. It is possible too that he may be unconsciously attracted to Beatrice and so offers the proposal in a spirit very like that of Beatrice's complaint – tossed off casually but signalling, and perhaps bringing suddenly to awareness, deep but previously unacknowledged feelings. Nor is the nature of Beatrice's response to the proposal any less ambiguous. Does she see it merely as banter and reject it in similar spirit? Or does she see it as banter and feel the hurt of being treated so casually, of being offered a proposal she is socially obligated to reject? Her 'silence' (II. i. 344) in the face of the offer may suggest an inner conflict of some sort. Does she for a moment seriously think about accepting? Does she think the proposal is genuine and turn it down in a kind of reflex action, prompted by pride and her habit of turning 'every man the wrong side out' (III. i. 68)? Or finally, does she think Don Pedro in earnest and reject him because she subconsciously still hopes to win Benedick?

Such varied interpretations would have to be narrowed by a production of *Much Ado About Nothing*, which could not present this full a range of possible meanings in the scene. But the text of the play will variously support all of these interpretations, because the actions and characters of the Prince and Beatrice periodically give hints of an emotional complexity full enough, 'real' enough, to make any of these explanations at least possible. All of which brings me back to my initial argument: the world of *Much Ado About Nothing* often seems more realistic, and less certainly interpretable, than any of the other worlds so far encountered in this study. And I take that quality to be a defining characteristic of the play, a sign that for the first time in his comedies Shakespeare sees his medium as extending beyond his immediate control, assuming a life that the playwright cannot altogether circumscribe, containing meanings that he cannot limit absolutely. In short, *Much Ado About Nothing* is the first Shakespearean comedy in which the dramatic world does not seem always fully subjected to the playwright's powers. For some of the characters, once called into being by the playwright, periodically take on a life of their own[2] and refuse to be treated like Margaret – as mere props to be moved mysteriously about and conjured up in various roles and costumes fashioned to the dramatic convenience of their creator.

To call a playwright a 'creator' in this context, however, is to emphasize the extent as well as the limitations of his achievement. By creating comic characters more fully human, more complex than he has produced in his comedies before, Shakespeare gives up some of his immediate control over them, so that we do not always feel the ubiquitous presence of the dramatist in his created world. We do not always feel him, in Kate's phrase, making puppets of his characters by manipulating them – literally playing with them – according to his dramatic will. But in giving up this kind of control over his characters the playwright, now 'creator,' also *extends* his dramatic powers in another way. He creates characters, vitalized by a dramatic life of their own, who do not always seem to move woodenly under the hands of the puppet-master. Instead they sometimes seem to answer the demands of their own wills and act upon humanly complex motivations. To be sure, this kind of realism is not altogether absent from the earlier comedies: we have noted it at times in Berowne, Petruchio, and Kate. But none of these characters remains consistently or even predominantly human. Berowne too often shows a surface of virtuoso verbal performances only: not even Rosaline can be sure of emotional depth in him; Petruchio plays the role of fairy tale hero so convincingly that he seems to possess more than human powers of perception and action; and Kate is long locked in the woodenness of her role as shrew before she is at last delivered into the fullness of human form by Petruchio – and Shakespeare. Nor is such realism everywhere indigenous to the world of *Much Ado About Nothing*:

Hero and Don John, to cite the most obvious examples, are no more complex as characters, and no less subject to the playwright's absolute control, than the two Antipholuses. But the same cannot be said of Don Pedro and Benedick, whose actions sometimes hint at a fullness of 'life' that seems to extend beyond the action of this play; or of Beatrice, who almost always seems complexly human.[3]

Almost as ambiguous and uninterpretable as her refusal of Don Pedro's hand, for instance, is her acceptance of Benedick's – not because her love for him comes as any surprise, since it has been apparent from her very first speech, but because it is so complexly embedded in a matrix of hatred. In the scene where Benedick declares his love to Beatrice and she secures his hand in a promised action against Claudio, love and hate are so interwoven in Beatrice's behavior that it is impossible to tell which emotion predominates:[4]

> *Beat.* You have stayed me in a happy hour: I was about to protest I loved you.
> *Bene.* And do it with all thy heart.
> *Beat.* I love you with so much of my heart that none is left to protest.
> *Bene.* Come, bid me do anything for thee.
> *Beat.* Kill Claudio. (IV. i. 285–91)

Is Beatrice here undergoing violent shifts of mood and irrationally jumping from feelings of love for Benedick to feelings of hatred for Claudio? Or is she pretending to love in order to make Benedick serve the purposes of her hatred? Or, more complexly, are her feelings of love and hate – both emotions of great power – so much alike in their intensity as to be almost interchangeable? Or are hate and love, emotions already complexly tangled in Beatrice's feelings about Benedick, now given further and fuller expression as a result of Claudio's betrayal of Hero? Does Claudio's action emotionally reactivate for Beatrice the experience of Benedick's earlier betrayal of her love, and so intensify her present anger about what has happened to Hero? The most appropriate mood for criticism of *Much Ado About Nothing* may be the interrogative, because so much of importance in the play proves conjectural. As audience, we are sometimes as bewildered and confused by its action as the characters are.

What most often produces confusion among the characters is the basic feelings of distrust that underlie almost every event and relationship in Messina. In this world characters, unusually sensitive to personal insult, are quick to see betrayals in the actions of people around them. Don John imagines Claudio has won the favor of Don Pedro solely at his expense; Claudio thinks first that Don Pedro and then that Hero have broken faith with him; Don Pedro supposes that, as stale, Hero makes a mockery of his position as prince and match-maker by marrying his friend under false pretenses. Of course, the characters do not feel distrust without some reason, because betrayal is a common occurrence in Messina. What is unreasonable about this distrust, however, is the way it is tied to impulses of violence. Characters who think they have been wronged regularly resolve to work terrible revenges on the wrong-doers, and often such resolutions, prompted by rage, carry the revengers to the edge of madness. Don John, whose irrational hatred knows no measure, would, if he were unmuzzled, bite all the world; Leonato, violently angered by the 'confirm'd' (IV. i. 152) promiscuity of his daughter, thinks of killing her; Claudio, humiliated, as he thinks, by being contracted in marriage to a stale, publicly damns her as a whore and then leaves her for dead before the marriage altar; and Beatrice, enraged by Claudio's villainous betrayal of Hero, swears that she would, if only she were a man, 'eat his heart in the market-place' (IV. i. 308–9). In Messina, then, we find a dark underside to human behavior, partly because we meet here, for the first time in this study, the conscious human villainy that is nearly always excluded from the early comedies and nearly always included in the later ones; but partly also because the impulses of the villain sometimes find expression in the behavior of well-intentioned characters as well – in their susceptibility to intense feelings of anger, their unmoderated desire to inflict hurt on others, their pride perversely sensitive to injury, and their peculiar fascination for making believe, for manipulating surfaces to deceptive purpose.

Much of the energy exhibited by the characters in *Much Ado About Nothing*, for example, has less to do with self-delighting play, with assimilating and manipulating reality, than it has to do with a self-defensive tendency to close out what seems alien and threatening. In this play characters often isolate themselves in make-believe worlds by turning away from facts and even at times from their own feelings. Beatrice, retreating from the pain of rejected love, makes believe, even to herself, that she holds Benedick in contempt; she isolates herself from her deepest feelings and pushes Benedick away with her stabbing wit. Benedick, locked in a superannuated adolescence and afraid to surrender the security of his accepted identity as 'one of the boys,' makes believe that he is an enemy to marriage; he closes himself off from what he most desires – marriage to Beatrice. Don John, longing in spite of his bastardy to be accepted as a brother by the Prince and as a prince by society, makes believe that he chooses to be 'disdained of all' (I. iii. 30); he isolates himself in the role of an outsider, who must buy friends and the services of loyal retainers. Make-believe does not always take such obvious or extreme forms in *Much Ado About Nothing*. It also appears, apparently harmlessly, in the wealth of ceremonies and niceties of conduct and manners which characterize life in Messina. But in a world where make-believe is an integral part of the social structure, where formulaic ceremonies and manners provide easy cover for deception, deceit almost naturally becomes an action of central dramatic concern: make-believe finds its supreme expression in making others believe.

And so the play comes ultimately to deal with problems of belief – with Don Pedro's deceptive practice for making Benedick and Beatrice believe that they love one another, with Don John's deceptive practice for making Claudio believe that Hero does not love him. Practice, deception, make-believe can be used for good or evil ends, and what is tested by such practices is man's capacity for belief, with its roots in trust and, finally, in faith. Claudio does not believe in Hero enough to doubt the evidence of his senses; Benedick believes so completely in Beatrice – surely her name in this context is significant – that he is willing to defend her word with his life, though she offers no evidence in answer to Don John's apparent proof of Hero's adultery. What *Much Ado About Nothing* thus presents as it plays through its variations upon the theme of making believe is the dramatic embodiment of a near biblical definition of faith, as 'the substance of things hoped for, the evidence of things not seen' (Heb. 11:1). It is therefore probably no accident that this comedy has as its principal lovers characters named Benedick and Beatrice, that its clown is unaccountably blessed with the capacity to work goodness, and that its most faithfully steadfast lover passes through a kind of symbolic death and resurrection. Make-believe in *Much Ado About Nothing* finally directs us to the question of what belief, in its ultimate expression as faith, is.

Opposing belief, which in this play involves trusting another person enough to take him fully and completely to the self, are the destructive forces of distrust, which isolate and divide one human being from another, and which find their essential expression – dramatically embodied and variously repeated in the climactic, aborted wedding scene – in an act of destructive uncreation. Demonically parodying the artist's act of creation, Don John, whose birth has been cursed by bastardy, brings into church and wedding the uncreating word:

> There, Leonato, take her back again . . . (IV. i. 32)

> Kill Claudio. (IV. i. 291)

> Do not live, Hero; do not ope thine eyes . . . (IV. i. 125)

> What should I speak?
> I stand dishonour'd, that have gone about
> To link my dear friend to a common stale. (IV. i. 64–6)

At the climactic center of *Much Ado About Nothing* we encounter not the joyous exuberance of assimilative play, fully and freely expressed, but the dark rage of distrust, biting at the world and spitting out, in the short, clipped, niggardly accents of hate, an eternal 'No.'

For this reason Claudio's act finally of accepting Leonato's 'niece' on faith, by taking her to him in marriage with only the word of her 'uncle' to establish her worth, has crucial thematic meaning: it signals his willingness for the first time to trust another person unreservedly; it is an expression of faith consciously embodied in action. So however mindless and precipitous, however uncaring and even mercenary Claudio's action here may seem from a realistic perspective, it is also thematically understandable as an act of faith – in Hero that is dead, in Leonato, and in the promise of marriage – which passes understanding and, in a sense, resurrects Hero for Claudio. Like Beatrice's earlier unquestioning trust in Hero's innocence or Benedick's unshakable faith in the correctness of Beatrice's judgment of Hero – 'Sweet Hero! She is wronged, she is slandered, she is undone.' (IV. i. 314–15) – it is a sign of one individual's willingness to trust another absolutely, to take him into the intimate world of the self without reservation or doubt, even in the face of apparent betrayal. It is, in short, an expression of faith in an almost Biblical sense, and it presents a marked contrast to the characters' habitual practice of taking others in, in a very different meaning of the phrase: namely, by deceiving them, often so that they may be violently pushed away from the self. A faith founded on a trust in others is too little valued – until near the end of the play – in the world of *Much Ado About Nothing*, where characters, acutely sensitive to the possibility of betrayal, put their trust in the hard, tangible evidence of the senses. What they would know for certain, they would see or hear: 'If you dare not trust that you see, confess not that you know . . . '(III. ii. 122–3). This fact may explain why characters who lack faith in friends or lovers may still believe the words of someone they have good reason to think is a villain. For Don John offers the apparent certainty of what can be heard and seen, as his false testimony against Hero repeatedly makes clear:

> go but with me to-night, you shall *see* her chamber-window entered . . . If you dare not trust that you *see*, confess not that you know: if you will follow me, I will *show* you enough; and when you have *seen* more and *heard* more, proceed accordingly. . . . I will disparage her no farther till you are my *witnesses*: bear it coldly but till midnight, and let the issue *show* itself. . . . O plague right well prevented! so will you say when you have *seen* the sequel. (III. ii. 115–37; my italics)

What Claudio forgets in his anger and haste to see proof of Hero's faithlessness, however, is how untrustworthy the evidence of his senses has already proved to be: when he earlier heard from both Benedick and Don John that Don Pedro was courting Hero for himself, he immediately saw what he thought were clear signs of such a courtship. And, he has only just finished playing out with Don Pedro and Leonato a dramatic production carefully designed to deceive the eyes and ears of Benedick, who trusts too quickly in what he sees and hears. But like Benedick in the garden, Claudio notices only the surface details of the dramatic production staged for him. He does not recognize that this drama is less than life-like, offering merely costumed figures seen through a glass darkly. Nor does he take into account what he knows about the probable nature of Don John's character. Nor finally, does he notice the obvious analogy between his situation under Hero's window and Benedick's in the garden. He forgets his responsibility as audience, to the action of both drama and life, to discover fullness of meaning and instead allows himself to be taken in by surface appearance – shadows. And although an audience watching *Much Ado About Nothing* cannot make Claudio's particular mistake, it may be meant to profit by his example: his error may serve to make that audience more aware of its identity *as* audience and, simultaneously, of its consequent responsibility not to take the surface of a dramatic production – or of life – for the whole. Instead that audience may be encouraged by Claudio's mistaking to 'mind' the play of life and art, to bring to it sound and sensitive critical faculties, which probe carefully beneath dramatic surfaces in an effort to discover fuller, and more complex, meanings.

Such complexity we have already discovered in *Much Ado About Nothing*, beneath the surface of the problems produced by Margaret's inconsistency, Don Pedro's proposal, and Beatrice's response to Benedick's avowal of love. To this list we might also add the tangled bundle of questions tied into the confusing beginning of the play. There we are first confused by three different versions of Don Pedro's plan for courting Hero, then misled by the characters' misinterpretations of this courtship once it is undertaken, and finally bewildered by the apparent collapse of the main plot, when this courtship comes to a seemingly tidy conclusion in the engagement of Hero and Claudio. Having gradually led us to believe that Don Pedro has fallen in love with Hero – since Don John, Claudio, and Benedick, who view the courtship from three radically different perspectives, all interpret it in this way – Shakespeare then summarily dissolves this belief with an anti-climax so casual that we wonder if we have been as mistaken as the characters. We wonder if we were supposed to know all along that Don Pedro never really abandons his original plan to court Hero for Claudio. As a way of introducing his audience to a dramatic world rife with uncertainty and distrust, then, Shakespeare arouses expectations which he afterwards casually dismisses, thereby encouraging his audience to distrust its responses and to feel uncertain about the validity of its expectations. The atmosphere of the dramatic world thus temporarily touches the audience, which experiences its own particularly appropriate kind of uncertainty and distrust about the world of *Much Ado About Nothing*.

That audience may also feel a kind of uncertainty about the playwright's control of his dramatic world, where his play-making powers are at once both extended and newly qualified. For at the beginning of *Much Ado About Nothing* Shakespeare seems to be renouncing obvious dramatic manipulation and turning away from play-making which calls attention to the artist's presence in his creation. Instead he creates characters whose human complexity makes them resistant to the playwright's imposing control; he makes his villain a manipulator – though an unimaginative one – whose manipulations are motivated by sadness rather than by joy; and he presents the manipulative activities of well-intentioned characters as misguided – as an unnecessary and often disruptive fascination with the power derived from using deceptive surfaces to advantage.[5] But in the process the action of Shakespeare's play goes nowhere.[6] After the first act and a half, the plot – both Don John's and Shakespeare's – apparently collapses. When given the freedom their fullness of being seems to demand, the characters refuse to submit to the dramatist's purposes; they will not allow the plot to develop the inevitable complications and ramifications necessary for a successful five-act play. Instead the characters easily resolve the problems precipitated by their own misunderstandings and Don John's schemings, and then they prepare for the wedding of Claudio and Hero.

Only barely begun, with the atmosphere of its world defined, its major characters introduced, and its complications of plot developing according to relatively predictable dramatic patterns, the play seems suddenly undone by its characters, who pursue their own interests rather than those of the playwright or the audience. With rebellious unconcern for the conventions of the theater, they cut through what appears to be the beginning of an intricate comic plot, and then prepare for a wedding which will apparently conclude this comedy and send the audience home – in the middle of the second act. So much for drama which eschews manipulation and allows its characters a life of their own. For these characters may prove as wilfully unmanageable, and their world as unassimilable to the dramatist's purposes, as real people and life itself.

In the first act and a half of *Much Ado About Nothing*, then, Shakespeare may be dramatically confronting again the problem he faced in the Induction to *The Taming of the Shrew*: namely, how to introduce into art the complex, often incoherent, energies of life; and as a corollary to this problem, how to assimilate life's apparent incoherence into the ordered, constricting forms of dramatic convention. In both plays Shakespeare seems to begin in partial rebellion against the conventional practices of his earlier play-making, as if he were searching for new possibilities in a dramatic form threatening to go stale for him. In *The Taming of the Shrew* this rebellion is obvious, because it is exuberantly announced in both literal and metaphorical dramatic violence. The action of the play, probably preceded by the crash of breaking glasses, begins with Sly on the run and then suddenly collapsed and abandoned – which is exactly the way the Induction proceeds dramatically: offering an almost endless series of beginnings which are hardly put in motion before they too collapse, and are abandoned by the playwright. In *Much Ado About Nothing*, on the other hand, Shakespeare's rebellion against conventional dramatic forms is neither so obvious nor so exuberant. The plot of the play begins like that of a conventional comedy, with the arrival of young men who quickly become romantically involved in the life of Messina; and the playwright seems partly to be forswearing the manipulative powers which he has earlier celebrated with such dramatic joy. That is what is unconventional about the beginning of *Much Ado About Nothing*: the new freedom and complexity it grants to some of its characters, and the attendant lessening of obvious manipulative control exercised by the dramatist over those characters.

In both *The Taming of the Shrew* and *Much Ado About Nothing*, however, Shakespeare's rebellion against convention ends in a kind of anticlimax: in one case, with an Induction abandoned only very shortly after it is at last coherently begun; in the other, with a play apparently concluded long before its duly appointed time. And in both plays, too, Shakespeare's attempt to get life into drama simultaneously both succeeds and fails. Into the conventional form of a play he manages temporarily to introduce, in the one case, the formless incoherence of life and, in the other, the bewildering complexity of 'real' characters, but eventually this kind of life proves incompatible with the constricting demands of drama – that its action should develop coherently, for instance; or that its plot should take five acts (or approximately two hours' traffic on the stage) to develop, complicate, and finally resolve itself. So the life assimilated into the conventional forms of drama eventually disrupts those forms, and interrupts the play. Then if the dramatist is to maintain coherent control over his work and abide by the incontrovertible convention of the theater that he *complete* his play, and in due time, he must impose more direct control over his plot and characters. He must do again what he has done so successfully before in his comedies – and perhaps sought to avoid doing as artistically repetitious at the beginning of *The Taming of the Shrew* and *Much Ado About Nothing*: he must obviously manipulate his plot and his characters to bring them to a conventionally appropriate end, to make them serve his dramatic purposes and satisfy the audience's expectations. Suddenly upon his created play world, whose life has partly resisted the forms of dramatic convention, he imposes the ordering form of more conventional dramatic action. And his way of beginning to do so is literally to bring in more conventional dramatic action, in the form of a play-within-the-play. In *The Taming of the Shrew* this play takes the form of the production staged for Sly, which soon becomes Shakespeare's play, replacing the one he cannot apparently mold into coherent form in the Induction. In *Much Ado About Nothing* the play-within-the-play which announces the playwright's more direct manipulation of his dramatic world and characters is the garden scene, where Don Pedro tricks Benedick into thinking that Beatrice loves him. And while it does not, like the players' production in *The Taming of the Shrew*, obviously become Shakespeare's play, it does substantially alter the tone and direction of *Much Ado About Nothing*.

It first of all begins to subject the characters more directly to the playwright's imposing control, since it prepares for the union of Beatrice and Benedick. This union has, of course, been implicit in the comic structure of the play from its beginning, but it has been threatened by the premature ending the characters seem to be preparing for the play in its second act. As a consequence, the playwright has to intervene and more directly take over the task of bringing his feuding lovers together and driving his betrothed lovers apart: he subjects Benedick and Beatrice to the match-making trickery of Don Pedro; he subjects

Claudio to the marriage-breaking trickery of Don John. At the same time – and this is the second effect of the garden scene – he calls his audience's attention to his acts of intervention, by self-reflexively dramatizing them. For Don Pedro and Don John both advance their plots – and Shakespeare's – by staged dramatic productions which depend for their success upon careful manipulation of actors and audience as well. Don John offers his audience costumed actors playing out a dramatic scene in a prearranged and limited space, using gesture and perhaps prearranged dialogue (about this detail Shakespeare's play is ambiguous) to produce a particular effect. It is true that Don John's purposes are radically different from Shakespeare's, since he hopes his audience will mistake the play for reality in a way a theater audience never would. But his action, like the playwright's, seeks more than usual control over both an audience and a specifically delimited world.

In a similar way, but to a very different purpose than Don John's, Don Pedro's tricking of Benedick calls attention to the playwright's manipulation of his audience and his medium. For Don Pedro's plot to succeed, his dramatic production must also manipulate its audience into belief by a careful control of dramatic gesture, dialogue, and action, a fact which is repeatedly called to the audience's attention, both by the characters' intrusive remarks about Benedick's response to their play and by their delight in making yet another play within their play-within-the-play: a play-within-the-play-within-the-play. They describe a scene of Beatrice in love agony for Benedick, sitting down at night to compose letters which she dares not send him. In their dramatic creation, four levels removed from reality (since they claim to know of it only by report from Hero), they include details of setting, scene, costume, action, and even dialogue:

> ... she'll be up twenty times a night, and there will she sit in her smock till she have writ a sheet of paper: my daughter tells us all. ... O, she tore the letter into a thousand half-pence; railed at herself, that she should be so immodest to write to one that she knew would flout her; 'I measure him,' says she, 'by my own spirit; for I should flout him, if he writ to me; yea, though I love him, I should.' (II. iii. 135–51)

Don Pedro and his friends are not, however, the only ones who must manipulate Benedick if their play is to succeed. Shakespeare also must manipulate him, though not in the same way: Don Pedro must fit his play to Benedick's needs; Shakespeare must fit Benedick to the needs of his play. He must make him comply to his dramatic purposes, even if his way of securing compliance is not altogether consistent with Benedick's character as so far presented in the play. Here the demands of plot take precedence over those of character; so Shakespeare at least temporarily converts Benedick from a complex, convincingly human character almost to a puppet: in this scene he makes Benedick an ass, almost as limited in his perception of the meaning of what goes on around him as Dogberry will later prove to be. There is no other way to account for the absolute success of Don Pedro's – and Shakespeare's – scheme to make Benedick recognize his love for Beatrice. For the Benedick we have earlier encountered in this play would hardly have been so easily and completely taken in by Don Pedro's trick: it is too patently contrived, too particularly addressed to his hearing, and too obviously acted out, to be fully believed by any character with enough intelligence to be worthy of Beatrice's attention. Granted, Benedick is deceived partly because he *wants* to believe what he hears: he is already in love with Beatrice, even if he has not quite been willing to admit this fact, either to himself or to others. But even his predisposition to believe does not account for the manner of his submission here, for the laughably easy way in which he is fooled. That submission can, however, be explained by dramatic convention. In the theater, the gull submits absolutely to the most transparent of tricks. Which is precisely my point: in this scene Shakespeare converts a character who has earlier shown evidence of complex humanness into a conventional stage gull. He manipulates his character, conspicuously imposing control over him, to serve the interests of a conventional comic plot-line and a basic five-act play structure. At the same time Shakespeare calls dramatic attention to this manipulation: Benedick acts the part of the gull too willingly. Even his entrance, when he soliloquizes on the foolishness of those who fall victim to love's powers, is too obviously compliant to the dramatist's purposes. It is an entrance which acts as a kind of verbal dumb-show, introducing the scene by presenting a summary of the dramatic action to follow.

Then, finally, as if these effects were not sufficient to make the audience notice the imposition of the playwright's control upon his dramatic world and characters, Shakespeare presents, as the successor to this scene, its mirror image: the tricking of Beatrice, similarly reduced out of human complexity, and similarly deceived with unimaginable ease by a staged story of another's love for her. What an audience may have missed of the dramatist's intervention in the gulling of Benedick, it can hardly ignore in the obviously manipulative eavesdropping scene which follows; for this second scene of trickery seems an almost mechanical repetition of the first. Here not only Beatrice but also the other characters seem puppet-like as they woodenly repeat their own modified version of the scene we have just watched. In these two garden scenes, then, Shakespeare not only begins to impose a puppet-master's control on characters who often previously have seemed to move with a life of their own; he also calls dramatic attention to his imposition of such control.

The first of these actions has a clearly recognizable purpose: suiting the play to basic theatrical conventions of form and length. The second action, whose purposes are much less clear and a good deal more complicated, serves as a defining characteristic of Shakespearean comedy, where it variously signals the playwright's joy in his manipulative powers, awakens the audience's critical faculties by producing emotional detachment from the action of the play, draws the audience's attention to a similar kind of imposed control by a character, and disarms criticism of contrived comic actions and characters by openly admitting to such contrivance. In addition, Shakespeare's manipulation of his characters here announces that he has met the challenges of dramatic convention by assimilating them into the world of his play: for his way of imposing the constricting forms of a contrived plot on his characters in *Much Ado About Nothing* is partly to have his characters impose contrived plots on one another. In order to shape his play to the dictates of theatrical convention, Shakespeare makes his characters also shape plays, and although their purposes are radically different from his, their dramatic productions become the substance of his play.

The way is prepared for the eventual union of Benedick and Beatrice by the two staged plays that Don Pedro designs, and others help him to carry out. Then Hero and Claudio are driven apart (and Shakespeare's plot appropriately complicated) by the dramatic production Borachio conceives and Don John executes with help from Borachio and Margaret. When Claudio next stages his dramatic rejection of Hero before the church altar during their 'wedding' ceremòny, Shakespeare provides his plot with the further complication of Hero's apparent death, to which the Friar, suggesting a play that Leonato and Hero's friends can stage for the world at large and for Claudio in particular, gives form.[7] Finally, both the love plots are resolved by Leonato's elaborately staged drama of Claudio's wedding to his 'niece' which resurrects Hero and reunites her with Claudio, at the same time that it provides the natural setting for the betrothal of Benedick and Beatrice. All this is to say nothing of other actions in the latter half of the play which, while not exactly staged productions, appear as self-conscious dramatic performances: Dogberry's charge to the Watch and his official examination of the prisoners, Borachio's drunken re-creation for Conrade of the scene he has just finished playing with Margaret, Beatrice's possible dramatic manipulation of Benedick in order to secure his hand in a duel against Claudio, Antonio's railing against the corruption of 'Scrambling, out-facing, fashion-monging boys' (V. i. 94), and Benedick's solemn confrontation of, and challenge to, Claudio.

Much Ado About Nothing, then, abounds in dramatic performances, but these performances do not affirm the playwright's powers or the possibilities of his medium as exuberantly as they are affirmed in the earlier comedies – because no character in this world, no artist figure, like Oberon or Petruchio, presides for very long or very successfully over the play of others. For example, the principal figure of the artist within the play world, Don Pedro, acts with fitful success and generally diminished powers, a fact which makes him seem almost a minor character: he does not conspicuously seize our attention, as Petruchio or Oberon did or as Beatrice and Benedick do. He is often on stage, and he is touched by most of the major action of the play, but only occasionally does he occupy a place of central dramatic importance – when he proposes to Beatrice, when he brings forward his scheme for uniting the warring lovers, and when he turns away from Leonato's plea for support during the first wedding scene. Because he so often appears in the company of Claudio and/or Benedick, whose experiences provide the basis for the two major plots of the play, Don Pedro seems a supporting, not a major character. And then, too, his general demeanor keeps him from being conspicuous. He seems older, quieter, more self-contained than the characters he accompanies, and he rarely reveals to the other characters, or to us, what he actually feels: he has no soliloquies in the play, and no moments of clear, emotional self-revelation, except when he shows his proud sensitiveness to the insult Hero and Leonato have apparently paid to his position as Prince by encouraging him 'To link my dear friend to a common stale' (IV. i. 66).

In Don Pedro's bearing, then, we find a formality, a concern with proper princely behavior, which makes him often emotionally impenetrable: we cannot, for example, tell if he is at all romantically interested in the two most conspicuous young women of Messina, in spite of the fact that he courts one and proposes to the other. It is this formality that Beatrice identifies as her principal reason for refusing his offer of marriage: 'your grace is too costly to wear every day' (II. i. 341–2). Such a description suggests that Don Pedro lacks the quality most often associated with the artist figure in Shakespeare's earlier comedies – an apparently unbounded capacity for exuberant and spontaneous play. And because he lacks this quality, he seems eventually cut off from the joy of the play's happy ending: he ends as an outsider to the love which joins Benedick and Beatrice as well as Hero and Claudio – a fact which Benedick very particularly emphasizes:

> Prince, thou are sad; get thee a wife, get thee a wife: there is no staff more reverend than one tipped with horn. (V. iv. 124–6)

Although Don Pedro's play may have contributed to the making of the lovers' happiness, he himself seems finally excluded from such happiness.

Such a conclusion also calls to our attention the fact that Don Pedro has been essentially an outsider to the play's central action throughout: courting Hero off-stage where we do not see him and in such an ambiguous way as to confuse both the characters and us about his motives; conceiving the plan for bringing Benedick and Beatrice together and then appearing almost as an outsider in his own stage production, where Leonato and Claudio enthusiastically act out their tales of Beatrice's longing after Benedick; arriving, again off-stage, for the scene of Margaret's impersonation of Hero, which is never presented *in* Shakespeare's play and which Claudio and Don Pedro, as a corroborating witness (again a kind of outsider), view from a distance; and finally, watching, but not actively participating in, the love unions which complete the play.

By drawing attention to Don Pedro's identity as at least partly an outsider to the action of the play, Shakespeare may be dramatizing reservations he is beginning to feel about his art and about the relationship between it and reality. He may be dramatically confronting the problem of recognizing that there are limits to his assimilative powers, that reality may sometimes successfully resist his attempts to play with it, even in art. No such problem seemed to bother him in *The Taming of the Shrew*, where Petruchio possesses the power to make fairy tales come true, or in *A Midsummer Night's Dream*, where Shakespeare continually draws attention to his all-assimilating playwriting powers, as a manipulator of plots, as a creator of parodies, and as a dramatic magician who turns the failures of others into his own spectacular successes. All within the world of these comedies magically submits to his control. But in *Much Ado About Nothing*, as we have seen, his characters sometimes seem to obey their own wills as well as the playwright's. In the process they temporarily disrupt the playwright's control of a conventional five-act, two-hour-long plot structure. The play world will not yield fully to the dramatist's powers; so Shakespeare attempts to assimilate this artistic difficulty, as he has others in the past, by dramatizing it: he makes Don Pedro, the surrogate playwright figure, partly an outsider – a witness to, almost as much as an actor in – his world. And he limits the Prince's vision and powers. Don Pedro may be able to see, beneath the covering surface of their hostility, that Benedick and Beatrice are perfectly suited for one another, but he cannot penetrate the false surface of Don John's solicitousness and see the villainous action beneath; he can stage a successful dramatic production to make Benedick recognize his love for Beatrice, but he is powerless, even as Prince, to right the wrong he and Claudio, deceived by Don John's staged play, have done to Hero.

The world of *Much Ado About Nothing* proves too complex, too unmanageable to be effectively controlled by an artist figure within the play; his powers work with full effectiveness only in a very specifically defined and isolated realm – in Leonato's garden (or orchard). There Don Pedro's staged play magically fools Benedick and prepares for his ultimate union with Beatrice, but outside of the closely confined world of the garden, the Prince possesses no magic. His courtship of Hero provides substance for Don John's divisive talk and temporarily alienates him from his friend. His proposal to the heroine – perhaps serious, perhaps merely a social gesture – meets with rejection, and suggests a failure either of power (if the proposal is offered in earnest) or of vision (if it is merely a gesture). He is taken in by Don John, and gives at least tacit approval to Claudio's cruel plan for publicly rejecting Hero at the altar. He keeps company afterwards with Claudio, as both of them tastelessly try to recapture the holiday spirit that previously characterized their behavior in Messina. And finally, he is partially excluded, perhaps in lonely sadness, from the joy of the marriage celebrations at the end of the play. For these reasons it is tempting to see Leonato's orchard, where Don Pedro's play proceeds with magical success, as an image of a lost paradise temporarily regained for the dramatist – as a place where his powers work magically, exuberantly, spontaneously to produce the kind of comic scene we associate with the earlier comedies: outrageously and entertainingly manipulative, like the plot of *The Comedy of Errors*; in a world set off temporarily from the disruptive, unlooked-for intrusions of reality, like the world of *Love's Labour's Lost*; clearly making its planned seduction of a rebel against love known beforehand to Shakespeare's audience, like Petruchio's action in *The Taming of the Shrew*; and presenting in a play-within-the-play a parodic version of the main plot (which also misleads an eavesdropping audience with a staged dramatic production), like the mechanicals' production in *A Midsummer Night's Dream*.

In the first garden scene, then, Shakespeare temporarily returns to the kinds of manipulative play-making that have characterized his earlier comedies; in its content and characterization the scene is not so mature or so complex as much of the rest of *Much Ado About Nothing*, but it is perhaps the funniest and most dramatically successful scene in the play. Whether it also presents a paradigm of an earlier dramatic 'paradise' now only sometimes accessible to the playwright, we cannot say for certain, but we see significant differences, in tone and dramatic sophistication particularly, between this scene and many other parts of the play. And those differences do point the way to distinctions between the early, exuberant comedies and the later,

less joyful ones. These differences are not, of course, absolute: no
Shakespearean comedy is free from suggestions of sadness,
violence, suffering, and even death, as the first moments of
Shakespeare's first comedy make clear; nor are the later comedies
like *Much Ado About Nothing, As You Like It,* and *Twelfth Night*
predominantly dark in mood, since they *are* comedies. But I find
these later, 'mature' plays generally different in tone from the
earlier ones: they seem less self-delighting, less exuberant about
their manipulativeness, less certain of their capacity to assimilate
the intrusive reality of theatrical conventions – in short, less
playful. That does not mean that forms of play are any less
important or noticeable in them; it means only that the forms
often become sophisticated, more tenuous, more devious, and
finally more self-defensive. Moreover, the tone of these plays
changes enough with the writing of *Much Ado About Nothing* so
that even the scene most obviously like those of the earlier
comedies has a dark underside.

That scene is, after all, part of a trick that is at least once
referred to as a 'trap' (III. i. 106) and has much in common with
Don John's destructive scheme for undoing Hero, a fact the play
keeps drawing to our attention. Early in the scene, for example,
Don Pedro speaks to the musician of his plans to have music the
next evening at Hero's chamber window. This speech reminds
us, partly by its general reference to visiting Hero on the next
evening and partly by verbal echo, of the scene immediately
preceding this one, in which Don John and Borachio lay plans for
their own divisive play-within-the-play. So even as Don Pedro
begins the play he has designed to bring Benedick and Beatrice
together, Shakespeare reminds his audience that Don John is
simultaneously using a similar kind of play-making to destructive purposes. This fact is further emphasized in the second
garden scene when Hero, speaking of the way she will dissuade
Benedick from his fruitless pining after Beatrice, says that she
will 'devise some honest slanders/To stain my cousin with . . .'
(III. i. 84–5). Behind Don Pedro's plot we see the shadowy
outlines of Don John's. We see also evidence of the violent
emotions that sometimes take control of characters in the world
of *Much Ado About Nothing*. Benedick's acutely critical reaction
to Balthazar's song suggests an aggressiveness perhaps induced
by guilt (since he apparently has behaved with Beatrice much as
men are said to behave in Balthazar's song – 'as deceivers ever').

More importantly, Claudio and Leonato, in describing Beatrice's love agonies, present her as driven to desperate action by frustrated love: 'my daughter is sometime afeard she will do a desperate outrage to herself...' (II. iii. 156–8). The action they describe has not, of course, occurred, but it is perfectly consistent with Beatrice's character, with the intensity of felt emotion she projects. As a consequence, what here seems comic may, like Don Pedro's kind of plot in the hands of Don John, later show a dark and destructive side. For Beatrice will eventually act with desperate outrage to seek Claudio's death. The powerful emotions that Don Pedro and his friends play with in this scene can also be turned, with almost tragic effect, against them. Behind the intense emotions that are, in the eavesdropping scene, a source of comedy, we see potential tragedy; behind Don Pedro's plan to bring Benedick and Beatrice together, we see Don John's plan to drive Claudio and Hero apart; behind Don Pedro, the surrogate playwright figure, we see Don John, a kind of perverse anti-artist, the demonic complement to his brother.

Like Don Pedro, Don John is a kind of outsider, set apart from others by his sadness, which in him has festered into madness. Like Don Pedro too, he has an easily injured sense of pride, and a fondness for practicing deception. But where Don Pedro's concerns are with creating social harmony, Don John's are with divisiveness. His dramatic production, which proceeds under the aegis of darkness, has as its purpose the inspiration of hate, not love. He would, if he could, turn the happiness of others to ruin, simply because there is no measure to his own sadness. And in another sort of dramatic world, not presided over by a dramatist who imposes a comic plot upon his characters, Don John might succeed – in the dress of Iago, for instance. But throughout *Much Ado About Nothing* Shakespeare imposes his manipulative control as obviously on Don John as he imposes it on Benedick and Beatrice in the eavesdropping scenes. And his way of imposing that control is to make Don John so puppet-like a character that he acts only as a kind of prop, which is moved about at the dramatic convenience of the playwright: he appears as a stage villain who never for a moment transcends his role as a stage villain. He is all surface. About him we are told almost nothing which would explain his rancorous hatred of society or his determination to do harm. He is, of course, a bastard, but little is made of this fact in the play, where his bastardy is not even mentioned until after he has made his final exit.[8] And he has lately fallen out with his brother and been supplanted in favor by Claudio. Whether his 'overthrow' (I. iii. 70) is connected with the war mentioned at the beginning of the play is uncertain, but it seems unlikely, since he is never spoken of as the enemy or treated as a captive. Neither is his freedom to come and go in Messina explained by any generous pardon from Don Pedro, as we would expect it to be if Don John had been a defeated rebel. What in fact really matters about Don John's villainy is that it *is* essentially unmotivated, mere motiveless malignity. It cannot really be explained or understood because it is, like much evil, illogical and incomprehensible. For an audience interested in *logical* human action Shakespeare gives vague hints about Don John's possible motives – bastardy, revenge for some earlier humiliation, jealousy of Claudio, angry retaliation against a community which has made him an outsider – but they are hints only and meant, like so much in this play, to lead the unwary listener into mistaking.

Almost nothing about Don John's villainy, in fact, is understandable, for his plan to work harm is as shallow as his motives. It is not his idea in the first place, and when it is introduced he barely considers it or wonders about its details. We never learn *how* Borachio manages to fashion the matter of Hero's absence or how Margaret can innocently participate in the scheme – if she *does* participate in it innocently – without exposing it as villainy at the first word she hears of Hero's tragedy. Even such a necessary detail of plot as the need to disguise Margaret in Hero's clothing goes unmentioned until Borachio includes it, almost as an afterthought, in his confession. But what is probably most unconsidered about Don John's scheme for deceiving Claudio and Don Pedro is its end. The purpose of the plot seems to be general evil-doing – 'to misuse the prince, to vex Claudio, to undo Hero and kill Leonato' (II. ii. 28–30) – and the really destructive harm in the plan is aimed at the innocents, Hero and Leonato, against whom Don John has no complaint. Again there is no logic to his evil action. In addition there is in his conduct a vague suggestion of reckless self-destructiveness. Don John thinks nothing of how to protect himself from discovery after the plot is put into practice. He hears of an evil plan and embraces it with relish, never thinking on its possible consequences, as his subsequent self-incriminating flight makes clear. The details and ends of the plan are unimportant to Don John because he is attracted simply by the evil in it, not by its specific purpose. 'Grow this to what adverse issue it can, I will put it in practice' (II. ii. 52–3), he announces, and he does not care if the 'adverse issue' includes his own ruin. His interest is in doing evil, even if he himself may also be its victim.

Even evil, then, is reduced to a kind of make-believe form in Messina. It is bodied forth in a stage villain who thinks and acts only to do harm – motivelessly, purposelessly – as if the incomprehensible evil of man's world could, like some sort of ultimately destructive virus, be isolated and identified in a single organism. In the world of *Much Ado About Nothing* Don John gets almost all the blame, and is promised all the punishment, for disrupting the order of things. But to explain away the complexity of evil by locating it all in Don John and planning brave punishments 'tomorrow' is to forget that qualities associated with Don John inhere in modified forms in nearly everyone in Messina. Sometimes this tie with Don John is direct and obvious. Borachio conceives the plan for deceiving Claudio, Margaret helps him to carry it out, and Conrade delights in the report of it. But more often the correspondences are less recognizable, though no less important. Don Pedro, linked to Don John by ties of blood, shares with him both a propensity for practicing deceptions upon others and an easily injured sense of self-importance. Leonato, Claudio, and Beatrice all, at one time or another, seek revenge on those they think have wronged them. And Benedick, puffed up with pride when he enters Messina, shows his misguided sense of self-sufficiency by railing against marriage. But although the evil isolated and embodied in Don John inheres, less obviously, in almost all of the other characters in *Much Ado About Nothing*, no one recognizes this correspondence. No one has to, because Shakespeare's Messina is a comic not a tragic world. There passions unacknowledged or suppressed may erupt and threaten harm; there deceptive surfaces may disguise malicious intentions, and there the atmosphere may be clouded by deceit, eavesdropping, and false reports obscuring truth almost beyond recognition. Momentarily we may glimpse the shadowy outlines of a world like Hamlet's Denmark, but in doing so we are only again jumping to conclusions and mistaking, because in Messina the worst finally returns to laughter. All mistakes are either fortuitous or reversible. All problems at last come to nothing, to 'Hey nonny, nonny.' In Messina man is ultimately delivered from evil, both within and without.

What delivers him is the imposing control of the playwright operating through the unimposing form of Dogberry,[9] who is a kind of thematic complement to Don John. Like the Bastard he has been made an outsider from social importance by an accident of his birth – he is not a nobleman – and by past events – he is 'a fellow that hath had losses' (IV. ii. 85). But unlike Don John, he does not feel bitter or separated from the social community. Quite the contrary. He has readily acclimatised himself to his subordinate position in society by obsequiously serving his superiors and by expecting a similar sort of exaggerated deference from his underlings. His charge to the watchmen, specifying particularly that 'the watch ought to offend no man' (III. iii. 86–7), presents careful instructions about how to avoid disturbing the regular routine of life in Messina. And his favorite expression of address to subordinates, 'neighbor,' suggests a patronizing solicitousness of those less fortunate than he. Also like Don John, Dogberry is proud and has an easily injured sense of his own importance. But he finds a very different way of satisfying his wounded pride than the Bastard does. Don John keeps his bitterness pent up, biting it back to feed on its own rancor until it comes suddenly snarling into the open as malicious behavior. The Bastard's rigidly balanced, clipped speech, which suggests that he speaks through tightly clenched teeth, gives evidence of anger forcefully suppressed but barely controlled. Dogberry, on the other hand, knows nothing of forced suppression. His anger blows quickly to the surface and then harmlessly expends its energies in a series of spontaneous verbal explosions. Instead of biting at the world, Dogberry fulminates against it, and does no harm. Finally, Dogberry is related to Don John in being psychologically unexplainable, for as the Bastard is unaccountably evil in this play, the Constable is just as unaccountably good. Goodness may appear in Messina just as gratuitously as evil. There is no logical reason why Dogberry should be allied with, should in fact be the primary agent of, effective powers for goodness. He is vain, self-serving, and stupid. And he never even fully understands the nature of Borachio's crime, which he interprets variously as false knavery, flat perjury, burglary, and slander. He is, in fact, more disturbed by Conrade's accusation that he is an ass than he is by anything Borachio has done. But as confused as he is about what crime has been committed, Dogberry knows that the offenders look like knaves, and he stubbornly pursues the course of justice as he understands it. In the process he plays havoc with due process, wilfully misinterprets testimony, and joins Claudio in the error of jumping to conclusions on the basis of imperfectly observed evidence. But although Dogberry constantly makes mistakes about particulars, he is never in error about the one fact that really matters, his judgment that the men before him are villains. As a consequence, he delivers the world of *Much Ado About Nothing* from tragedy.

And he effects this delivery both dramatically – by infusing the play with new comic energies – and thematically – by leading the people of Messina at last to the truth of Don John's slanders. Dogberry can accomplish such good because he is blessed. Shakespeare has given him, like so many of his clowns, enormous dramatic vitality; and if he seems to borrow some of his energy vicariously from Bottom, by imitating Bottom's self-importance, delight in life, malapropisms, asininity, and select but imperfect vision of truth, it may be because the playwright, finding limits to his creative energies, returns to a comic formula of proven worth. For Dogberry, like Bottom, is unknowingly not only an ass but a parodist. He reduces the problems of Messina to harmlessness by re-enacting them in the form of unconscious parodies. So he transmutes concern with artificial speaking, and other forms of false-seeming, into the ridiculousness of malapropism. So he turns potentially destructive self-importance and sensitivity to personal insult into mere matter for laughter, by railing pompously against one who has called him an ass. And so he mitigates the potentially tragic tone of Hero's wedding scene by providing an obvious parody of it in the scene which follows. There, in another kind of formal ceremony of examination, the usual order of things is interrupted by a self-important, self-assured interrogator who depends on the evidence of eavesdropping witnesses, makes false charges, and jumps to conclusions about guilt merely by judging the appearance of the accused.

But Dogberry is blessed not only in being infused with dramatic vitality. In addition his creator, or, from the perspective of the world he inhabits, his Creator, has blessed him in the most literal sense. For Dogberry is unaccountably tied to the powers of goodness. His first words are an inquiry about the essential worth of the men before him – 'Are you good men and true?' (III. iii. 1) – and his idiom is notable almost as much for its religious bias as for its malapropisms. The word 'God' appears twenty-two times in his speeches, more than a third of its total appearances in the play, and the basically religious tone of his talk is intensified by the use of words and phrases' like 'cursing hypocrite,' 'merciful,' 'piety,' 'excommunication' and 'redemption.' Of course, Dogberry has no clear understanding of what these words mean, but he is blessed by an intuitive capacity to work goodness. Like Bottom, who experiences a 'most rare vision,' Dogberry sees his way to truth in a world where others, a good deal less foolish than he, fall into potentially tragic error. And in Messina this truth, this wise foolishness, finally sets the other characters free, delivering them from near tragedy into the happiness of the comic ending that Shakespeare has promised, in its due time, since the first eavesdropping scene.

Concluding Remarks

At the end I return to the argument of my beginning: because Shakespeare's later comedies, from *The Merchant of Venice* to *Twelfth Night*, are in some significant ways different from their predecessors, in presenting characters of greater depth, poetry of greater range and sophistication, and worlds of greater complexity, they have long served as the model for Shakespeare's achievement as a comic dramatist. But in the process, they have also caused us to undervalue the early comedies, which we have seen primarily as preparations for the future. It is true that these plays do in part serve such a purpose; the experimental quality particularly of *The Comedy of Errors* and *Love's Labour's Lost* cannot be denied. But it is also true that the early comedies are unique as well as prophetic, for they celebrate an absolute self-assurance and joy in play-making. They announce Shakespeare's unqualified delight in discovering in the theater a world which seems fully manipulable by his imaginative powers – a child's play world made real and available to the playwright hero, whose capacity for play endows him with almost magical powers. None of Shakespeare's later works so conspicuously announces or so fully celebrates his joy in his own creative powers, in the theatrical medium, and in the act of play-making itself as these early comedies.

Just how the exuberant optimism of the early works is qualified by the vision of Shakespeare's mature comedies is clearest in *Much Ado About Nothing*. For in this work the powers of the artist figure are noticeably diminished. Instead of Petruchio, whose energy for life and play transforms the world about him, or Oberon, whose magic brings the order of a happy ending out of seemingly disparate plots and circumstances, *Much Ado About Nothing* gives us Don Pedro, whose success as a play-maker and world-shaper is much more limited. In addition his actions are subject to corrupting influences, since the Prince is shadowed by the figure of his bastard brother, who uses his play-making powers to perverse purpose: as Don Pedro stages dramatic performances to bring lovers together, Don John uses them to drive lovers apart. The powers of a playwright, Shakespeare here suggests, may be turned as much to deception as to vision, as much to destruction as to creation.

And as the playwright's powers may assume distorted forms, so also may play itself. In *Much Ado About Nothing* play appears most noticeably as make-believe, often thrown up as a defense against the unassimilable facts of reality. Beatrice makes believe that she does not love Benedick, because that love promises only sorrow: he has apparently jilted her in the past, and his resolution to die a bachelor seems to preclude any possibility of satisfying that love in the future. Similarly, Benedick makes believe that he does not love Beatrice, because his love for her threatens his defining independence, his publicly proclaimed identity as a man too wise to trust in the empty conventionality of marriage. In *Much Ado About Nothing* play, as make-believe, is as much defensively extrusive as assimilative, for repeatedly the characters push reality away from them, insulating themselves from fact and even from their own feelings by clinging doggedly to their distinctly selective, incomplete, and often distorted world-views. That is partly why the action of the play focuses so often on instances of mis-hearing and mis-seeing – to emphasize the incompleteness, the selectively distorting quality, of the make-believe world-views constructed by the characters. That is also why the most conspicuous human gesture in the play, repeated with the regularity of obsession and dramatically epitomized in Claudio's treatment of Hero at the altar, is the act of pushing other people away, either physically or verbally. So the defensiveness of make-believe in *Much Ado About Nothing* shades into aggressiveness – Beatrice 'speaks poniards, and every word stabs' (II. i. 254) – and aggressiveness shades into destructiveness – Don John and Borachio stage a make-believe scene of sexual betrayal 'to misuse the prince, to vex Claudio, to undo Hero and kill Leonato' (II. ii. 28–9).

Granted, play is not always defensive or destructive in the world of *Much Ado About Nothing*; Don Pedro's production in the garden proves that play may still produce revelation as well as delusion or division. But the principal dramatic action of this work, focusing on Don John's staged indictment of Hero, turns play to potentially disruptive and destructive effect. True,

Shakespeare is merely playing with the problem of evil in *Much Ado About Nothing*. Don John is only a cardboard villain, no more psychologically believable than the wicked brothers of fairy-tale convention; and in addition his agents are apprehended even before Don John disrupts Hero's wedding. But although the forces of evil, turning play to destructive uses, finally fail to work out their purposes in Messina, we do feel their presence there and recognize that it is only the playwright's obvious intervention – in making Don John so formulaically tied to evil, in making Dogberry so fortuitously tied to goodness – which keeps them from succeeding. In this world there is no wholly successful ectype of the artist, no Petruchio or Oberon, who can shape reality to his desires. Instead the playwright must intervene from above, rather than through, his play world, which is now separate from him, containing no agent with his assimilative powers.

In *Much Ado About Nothing*, then, we find the dramatic fullness and maturity – in characterization, language, and most of all in complexity of world-view – which is a defining characteristic of the later comedies. For here all reality does not submit to the play-maker's almost magical energies and powers. Instead it variously resists his attempt to assimilate it both within the play world and within the wider world which contains the play. Such a view of the relationship between the possibilities of art and the intractability of reality is, of course, more mature than the exuberantly optimistic view presented in the early comedies. After all, what is maturity if it is not learning that the triumphs of youth, born of an energy which sometimes converts challenges to child's play, prove either temporary or illusory? The 'most rare vision' of the early plays, clearly the product and reflection of Shakespeare's 'youth' as a dramatist, yields eventually to the more qualified perspective of his dramatic maturity. From the fairy-tale world of *The Taming of the Shrew* and the fairy world *A Midsummer Night's Dream* we pass inevitably, in *Much Ado About Nothing*, into a realm both more complex and less conformable to human desires. But it is worth noting, before we deprecatingly dismiss these early comedies as unimportant because they are 'immature,' that, in their exuberant celebration of the human capacity to master reality by playing with it, they present us with a dramatic world no less true to human emotional experience than the world of the later comedies. Less abiding, unfortunately, but no less true.

Notes and References

INTRODUCTION

1. See Northrop Frye, *A Natural Perspective* (New York: Columbia University Press, 1965) particularly ʾpp. 2–10.
2. In addition to Frye, see also Howard Felperin, *Shakespearean Romance* (Princeton University Press, 1972) and Barbara A. Mowat, *The Dramaturgy of Shakespeare's Romances* (Athens: University of Georgia Press, 1976).
3. This argument, as concerns particularly Shakespeare's later plays, is cogently presented by Robert Egan in *Drama Within Drama* (New York: Columbia University Press, 1975). See particularly pp. 9–14, 118–19.
4. See particularly Erving Goffman, *The Presentation of Self in Everyday Life* (Garden City: Doubleday Anchor, 1959) and Elizabeth Burns, *Theatricality* (New York: Harper and Row, 1972).
5. Anne Righter, *Shakespeare and the Idea of the Play* (London: Chatto and Windus, 1962).
6. Sidney Homan, 'When the Theater Turns to Itself,' *New Literary History*, 2 (Spring 1971) 407–17.
7. Johan Huizinga, *Homo Ludens* (Boston: Beacon Press, 1955) p. 28.
8. For an interesting discussion of this critical problem see Robert Weimann, 'Shakespeare and the Study of Metaphor,' *New Literary History*, 6 (Autumn 1974) 149–67.
9. In addition to Anne Righter's and Robert Egan's books already mentioned, other full-length studies having much to do with play in Shakespeare include: C. L. Barber, *Shakespeare's Festive Comedy* (Princeton University Press, 1959); James L. Calderwood, *Shakespearean Metadrama* (Minneapolis: University of Minnesota Press, 1971); and Alvin Kernan's book-length section on Renaissance plays and playwrights in Clifford Leech and T. W. Craik (eds.), *The Revels History of Drama in English*, vol. 3 (London: Methuen, 1975), pp. 237–508. Of particular notice too are the following studies of play in specific comedies: Michel Grivelet, 'Shakespeare, Moliere, and the Comedy of Ambiguity,' *Shakespeare Survey*, 22 (1969) 15–26; Richard Henze, 'Role Playing in *The Taming of the Shrew*,' *Southern Humanities Review*, 4 (Summer 1970) 231–40; and D. J. Palmer, '*As You Like It* and the Idea of Play,' *Critical Quarterly*, 13 (Autumn 1971) 234–45.
10. Friedrich Schiller, *On the Aesthetic Education of Man*, eds Elizabeth Wilkinson and L. A. Willoughby (Oxford: Clarendon Press, 1967) p. 107 (Fifteenth Letter).

11. The term is Erik Erikson's in *Childhood and Society*, 2nd ed. (New York: Norton, 1963): 'The *microsphere* – i.e. the small world of manageable toys – is a harbor which the child establishes, to return to when he needs to overhaul his ego' (p. 221).
12. Erikson, p. 212.
13. Jean Piaget, *Play, Dreams and Imitation in Childhood* (New York: Norton, 1962), particularly pp. 87–212.
14. Piaget, p. 147.
15. Piaget, p. 87.
16. Like all such omissions from studies of this kind, this one is perhaps arbitrary. I suspect that somewhere I could find a Shakespearean who feels about *The Two Gentlemen of Verona* as I feel about *The Taming of the Shrew*: that it is a masterpiece which has never had its proper due from critics, who have conspicuously omitted it from important studies of the comedies or the early plays. To this Shakespearean I tender my apologies, with the mitigating excuse that *The Taming of the Shrew* has a long history of stage success to recommend it, while *The Two Gentlemen of Verona*, at least in my experience, does not work any better on the stage than on the page.

CHAPTER 1

1. See Bertrand Evans, *Shakespeare's Comedies* (Oxford: Clarendon Press, 1960) pp. 1–9, for a detailed presentation of this argument.
2. A similar argument is made by A. C. Hamilton, *The Early Shakespeare* (San Marino: Huntington Library, 1967) pp. 103–4.
3. All references to Shakespeare in this study are from the edition of Hardin Craig, *The Complete Works of Shakespeare* (Chicago: Scott, Foresman, 1951).
4. The most interesting and developed statement of this idea, particularly as it applies to the comedies, is Maynard Mack's, 'Engagement and Detachment in Shakespeare's Plays,' in *Essays on Shakespeare and Elizabethan Drama in Honor of Hardin Craig*, ed. Richard Hosley (Columbia, Missouri: University of Missouri Press, 1962) pp. 275–96.
5. For a full discussion of this idea, see Leo Salingar, *Shakespeare and the Traditions of Comedy* (Cambridge University Press, 1974) pp. 59–67.
6. See Michel Grivelet, 'Shakespeare, Moliere, and the Comedy of Ambiguity,' *Shakespeare Survey*, 22 (1969) pp. 15–26, for a discussion of this theme in *The Comedy of Errors* and of its relation to the work of Moliere.
7. Exploration beyond the immediate boundaries of the play, though, does not always have to seem as misguided as L. C. Knights makes it sound in 'How Many Children Had Lady Macbeth?' *Explorations* (New York: George W. Stewart, 1947) pp. 15–54. Often a play encourages such speculation as a way of understanding present actions, as I hope to show later in a quasi-psychological analysis of Kate.
8. See particularly R. A. Foakes' 'Introduction' to the New Arden edition of *The Comedy of Errors* (London: Methuen, 1962) p. xlii, and Harold Brooks 'Themes and Structure in *The Comedy of Errors*,' *Early Shakespeare*,

Stratford-upon-Avon Studies 3, eds John Russell Brown and Bernard Harris (London: Edward Arnold, 1961) p. 65.

9. A similar argument is made by Hugh M. Richmond in *Shakespeare's Sexual Comedy* (Indianapolis: Bobbs-Merrill, 1971) pp. 50–1.

10. This argument is presented in a somewhat different form by Ralph Berry in *Shakespeare's Comedies* (Princeton University Press, 1972) p. 36. A more general statement about the thematic importance of money in comedy appears in Thomas McFarland's *Shakespeare's Pastoral Comedy* (Chapel Hill: University of North Carolina Press, 1972) pp. 15–16.

CHAPTER 2

1. See Rosalie L. Colie, *Shakespeare's Living Art* (Princeton University Press, 1974) p. 31.

2. For a thorough discussion of the pastoral elements in *Love's Labour's Lost* see Thomas McFarland, *Shakespeare's Pastoral Comedy* (Chapel Hill: University of North Carolina Press, 1972) pp. 49–77.

3. The most notable examples of this argument, presented in one way or another by almost every critic of the play, include: Ralph Berry, *Shakespeare's Comedies* (Princeton University Press, 1972) pp. 72–88; A. C. Hamilton, *The Early Shakespeare* (San Marino: Huntington Library, 1967), pp. 128–42; and Stanley Wells, 'Shakespeare Without Sources,' *Shakespearian Comedy*, Stratford-upon-Avon Studies 14, eds Malcolm Bradbury and David Palmer (New York: Crane, Russak, 1972) pp. 58–74.

4. It is, S. K. Heninger, Jr claims, in 'The Pattern of *Love's Labour's Lost*,' *Shakespeare Studies*, 7 (1974), 'the simplest plot in all Shakespeare' (p. 38).

5. Molly Mahood, *Shakespeare's Wordplay* (London: Methuen, 1957) p. 164.

6. For a similar argument see James L. Calderwood, *Shakespearean Metadrama* (Minneapolis: University of Minnesota Press, 1971) pp. 56–7.

7. Similar observations are made by Calderwood, p. 78; Herbert R. Coursen, Jr, '*Love's Labour's Lost* and the Comic Truth,' *Papers on Language and Literature*, 6 (Summer 1970) p. 320; and A. C. Hamilton, p. 133.

8. This idea is borrowed in part from Calderwood, p. 78.

9. Bobbyann Roesen makes the same argument in her essay on the play, '*Love's Labour's Lost*,' *Shakespeare Quarterly*, 4 (October 1953) p. 424.

10. J. J. Anderson in 'The Morality of *Love's Labour's Lost*,' *Shakespeare Survey*, 24 (1971) pp. 55–62, making a related argument, writes of Mercade: 'His sudden arrival, brief announcement, and immediate fading from view again suggest something of the medieval personified Death itself, coming like a thief in the night', p. 60.

11. For a comprehensive study of this convention in epic poetry see, Thomas M. Greene, *The Descent From Heaven* (New Haven: Yale University Press, 1963). See particularly p. 7.

12. At least that is how I think Mercade's entrance should work. During the hubbub produced by the announcement of Jaquenetta's pregnancy, the actor playing Mercade should enter unnoticed, probably near the back of the stage. Only gradually do the characters, one or two at a time, become aware of this outsider, dressed in black and perhaps hooded. As they notice him, the characters grow silent and draw back a step or two: slowly the

noise on the stage dies out, in one scattered group at a time, and the
characters stepping back from Mercade eventually give the audience its first
unobstructed view of him just as the stage becomes deathly quiet. Mercade
thus seems to have materialized suddenly, threateningly, in the very midst
of things.

13. This argument is made by Gates K. Agnew, 'Berowne and the Progress of
Love's Labour's Lost,' *Shakespeare Studies*, 4 (1968) p. 42.

14. Agnew, p. 44.

15. See particularly S. K. Heninger Jr, p. 45; Robert G. Hunter, 'The Function
of the Songs at the End of *Love's Labour's Lost*,' *Shakespeare Studies*, 7 (1974)
p. 61; and Hugh M. Richmond, *Shakespeare's Sexual Comedy* (Indianapolis:
Bobbs-Merrill, 1971) p. 80.

CHAPTER 3

1. The studies I refer to are: John Dover Wilson, *Shakespeare's Happy Comedies*
(Evanston: Northwestern University Press, 1962); Thomas McFarland,
Shakespeare's Pastoral Comedy (Chapel Hill: University of North Carolina
Press, 1972); and C. L. Barber, *Shakespeare's Festive Comedy* (Princeton
University Press, 1959). Wilson actually makes a passing admission that
The Taming of the Shrew belongs in his category but then ignores it anyway,
as 'only Shakespeare's in part' (p. 37).

2. James L. Calderwood, *Shakespearean Metadrama* (Minneapolis: University
of Minnesota Press, 1971). Although Calderwood does not discuss *The
Taming of the Shrew*, his analysis of the metadramatic elements of
Shakespeare's early plays has significantly influenced my interpretation of
this work: I am much in his debt.

3. A. C. Hamilton, *The Early Shakespeare* (San Marino: Huntington Library,
1967) and *Early Shakespeare*, Stratford-upon-Avon Studies 3, eds. John
Russell Brown and Bernard Harris (London: Edward Arnold, 1961).
Hamilton briefly explains his omission: 'I exclude *The Taming of the Shrew*
because the other comedies sufficiently show the pattern set up by these
early plays' (p. 7). Brown and Harris deal implicitly with the exclusion of
The Taming of the Shrew by explaining that the central focus of their
collection is three plays 'written around 1595 and 1597' – *Romeo and Juliet*,
Richard II, and *The Merchant of Venice* (p. 7).

4. The classification which most often does include *The Taming of the Shrew* is
romantic comedy. Peter G. Phialas in *Shakespeare's Romantic Comedies*
(Chapel Hill: University of North Carolina Press, 1966) and Hugh M.
Richmond in *Shakespeare's Sexual Comedy* (Indianapolis: Bobbs-Merrill,
1971) both discuss the play. But even in this category the status of *The
Taming of the Shrew* is uncertain. It is not, for instance, included in
Discussions of Shakespeare's Romantic Comedy, ed. Herbert Weil, Jr (Boston:
Heath, 1966), or in John Vyvyan, *Shakespeare and the Rose of Love* (London:
Chatto and Windus, 1960).

5. For a full discussion of this problem see Peter Alexander, 'The Original
Ending of *The Taming of the Shrew*,' *Shakespeare Quarterly*, 20 (Spring
1969), 111–16; and Richard Hosley, 'Sources and Analogues of *The Taming
of the Shrew*,' *Huntington Library Quarterly*, 27 (May 1964), 289–308; and

'Was there a "Dramatic Epilogue" to *The Taming of the Shrew?' SEL*, 1 (Spring 1961) pp. 17–34.

6. See John Dover Wilson, 'The Copy for *The Taming of the Shrew*,' The Cambridge Shakespeare *The Taming of the Shrew*, eds. Sir Arthur Quiller-Couch and J. D. Wilson (Cambridge University Press, 1928) pp. 97–126, particularly pp. 124–6.

7. This argument first appeared in 'The Argument of Comedy,' *English Institute Essays*, 1948, ed. D. A. Robertson Jr (New York: Columbia University Press, 1949) pp. 58–73.

8. I am borrowing an image here from Eugene Paul Nassar, *The Rape of Cinderella* (Bloomington: University of Indiana Press, 1970). Nassar's arguments about Shakespeare's manipulation of his audience and about the problems of discontinuity in literature, though they are sometimes opposed to what I have to say here, have significantly influenced my interpretation of *The Taming of the Shrew*.

9. *Aristophanes and the Comic Hero* (Cambridge, Mass.: Harvard University Press, 1964) pp. 25, 51.

10. The term is Whitman's, and he uses this modern Greek word to describe the essential qualities of Aristophanes' comic hero: '*Poneria* in modern Greek indicates not wickedness, but the ability to get the advantage of somebody or some situation by virtue of an unscrupulous, but thoroughly enjoyable exercise of craft. Its aim is simple – to come out on top; its methods are devious, and the more intricate, the more delightful . . . . [F]or though the word may be translated simply "cleverness," it also connotes high skill in handling those challenging aspects of life in which the agonistic tendencies of Greek psychology find a field of enterprise. It connotes further the qualities of protean resourcefulness and tenacity of purpose, and with all the world to gain, it can afford to dispense with any superfluous high-mindedness' (p. 30).

11. The defining characteristics of Old, as differentiated from New, Comedy are identified by Northrop Frye in 'Old and New Comedy,' *Shakespeare Survey*, 22 (1969) 1–5.

12. Sears Jayne, 'The Dreaming of *The Shrew*,' *Shakespeare Quarterly*, 17 (Winter 1966) 41–56.

13. For a careful analysis of this pattern see Cecil C. Seronsy, ' "Supposes" as the Unifying Theme in *The Taming of the Shrew*,' *Shakespeare Quarterly*, 14 (Winter 1963) 15–30.

14. This argument was first proposed, in a somewhat different way, by H. B. Charlton, *Shakespearian Comedy* (London: Methuen, 1938) p. 45: '*The Taming of the Shrew* is literally Shakespeare's recoil from romance.'

15. Anne Righter, *Shakespeare and the Idea of the Play* (London: Chatto and Windus, 1962) particularly p. 105.

16. There have been, of course, Inductions on the English stage before this one, but they have been concerned with introducing a theme or situation that will be directly explored in the play proper. This Induction, in contrast, generates its own autonomous dramatic world, and although it shares themes in common with the main play – uncertain and imposed identity, change of dress, violence, and war between the sexes – it is essentially independent of that play Thelma N. Greenfield in *The Induction in*

Notes and References

Elizabethan Drama (Eugene: University of Oregon Press, 1969) identifies such an Induction as a 'frame' and classifies *The Taming of the Shrew* with such works as *The Old Wives Tale, James IV,* and *Four Plays on Moral Representations in One,* which also have 'frames' for Inductions: 'With the frame, the actual stage holds two imaginative realms simultaneously... While one play envelops the other each has its own time, place, situation, and series of unfolding events' (p. 98). The Induction to *The Taming of the Shrew* is, however, only vaguely like the other 'frames,' since it has a uniquely explosive beginning, no ending, and an extended series of false starts, as I hope to show.

17. See Sherman Hawkins, 'The Two Worlds of Shakespearean Comedy,' *Shakespeare Studies,* 3 (1967) 62–80, an essay hardly noticed and yet perhaps the finest ever written about Shakespearean comedy.
18. Erik Erikson, *Childhood and Society,* 2nd ed. (New York: Norton, 1963) p. 214, quoting Schiller.
19. This idea and the concomitant importance of Sly's falling asleep are more fully discussed by Thelma N. Greenfield in 'The Transformation of Christopher Sly,' *Philological Quarterly,* 33 (October 1954) 34–42.
20. See Irving Ribner, 'The Morality of Farce: *The Taming of the Shrew,*' *Essays in American and English Literature Presented to Bruce Robert McElderry, Jr.,* ed. Max F. Schultz (Ohio University Press, 1967) pp. 165–76, particularly p. 171.
21. Robert Heilman in 'The *Taming* Untamed, or the Return of the Shrew,' *Modern Language Quarterly,* 27 (June 1966) 147–61, argues that this quotation is indicative of 'what farce does to all characters' (p. 155). Although he sees a different kind of symbolic meaning in the line than I do, his analysis first drew my attention to its importance.
22. Richard Henze in 'Role Playing in *The Taming of the Shrew,*' *Southern Humanities Review,* 4 (Summer 1970) 231–40, makes a corroborating argument: 'What Petruchio does, then, both during the wooing of Kate and the taming of Kate, is, like the Lord with Sly, to place his subject in a pageant where she will need an actor's ability to assess her role and decide how to play it. Unlike Sly, who remains a simple tinker because he lacks that ability, Kate finally learns, under the direction of Petruchio, to alter her role as the pageant of marriage and life requires', p. 234.
23. For obvious reasons of chronology Shakespeare could not have known *Grimm's Fairy Tales* particularly, but folk fairy tales, as Andrew Lang observes in the 'Preface' to *The Green Fairy Book* (New York: Dover, 1965) are among the oldest stories in the world.
24. *The Blue Fairy Book,* ed. Andrew Lang (New York: Dover, 1965) pp. 304–5.
25. Ibid., p. 308.
26. Bruno Bettelheim, 'The Uses of Enchantment,' *The New Yorker* (Dec. 8, 1975) p. 51
27. Ibid., p. 106.
28. Ibid., p. 90.
29. Joseph Campbell, *The Hero With a Thousand Faces* (New York: Meridian Books, 1956) p. 30.
30. I borrow this idea about the essential Shakespearean tragic action from

Bernard McElroy, *Shakespeare's Mature Tragedies* (Princeton University Press, 1973). McElroy, writing of the four great tragedies, begins: 'For all their diversity in tone and subject matter, Shakespeare's four mature tragedies, *Hamlet, Othello, King Lear*, and *Macbeth*, all embody at least one essential experience in common, the collapse of the subjective world of the tragic hero' (p. 3).

31. Campbell, *The Hero With a Thousand Faces*, p. 28.
32. Ibid., p. 29.
33. For the particulars of the Perilous Chapel episode in the grail quest, see Jesse L. Weston, *From Ritual to Romance* (Garden City: Doubleday Anchor, 1957) pp. 175–88.

CHAPTER 4

1. In the matter of effectiveness, for instance, Petruchio's counterpart in *A Midsummer Night's Dream* is not Bottom but Oberon. But that correspondence has to do with Petruchio's less conspicuous identity as playwright rather than as player.
2. This essay is indebted, more than I can say or would want to know, to the brilliant study of David Young, *Something of Great Constancy* (New Haven: Yale University Press, 1966). To identify every instance of my specific indebtedness to his work seems to me a fruitless exercise in cataloguing, since almost everything here is at least implicit in his argument. Suffice to say that I consider this reading merely a footnote to Young's work and that my most obvious borrowings from him (parenthetically followed by their location in his study) are in what I have to say about the playwright's self-consciousness (pp. 33–59, 69, 150–1), the dramatic moment as metaphor (p. 160), the metaphysical seriousness of Bottom's dream (pp. 115–26), the range of Shakespeare's language in the play (p. 86), and the relationship between Bottom and Oberon (p. 103).
3. Many of my ideas about the technical and thematic effects worked by a dramatic production of this play come from discussions with my colleague Wesley Morris, who has directed it.
4. Renaissance ideas about the limitations of intellect in achieving knowledge and about the consequent significance of blind Cupid as a symbol for both sacred and profane love – all immediately pertinent to my argument here and to Helena's soliloquy at the end of I. i. – are carefully explored and documented by Edgar Wind in *Pagan Mysteries in the Renaissance*, rev. ed. (New York: Norton, 1968) pp. 53–80.
5. For the way in which Shakespeare thematically fuses these two apparently contradictory festival times, see C. L. Barber, *Shakespeare's Festive Comedy* (Princeton University Press, 1959) pp. 119–39.
6. Whose wedding it was we probably can never know; but there is almost unanimous critical agreement that this play was originally written for a marriage celebration. See the Variorum Edition, ed. H. H. Furness (Philadelphia: J. B. Lippincott, 1895) pp. 259–64.
7. This idea as a predominant concern in Shakespearean comedy as a whole is interestingly examined in Hugh M. Richmond, *Shakespeare's Sexual*

Comedy (Indianapolis: Bobbs-Merrill, 1971). See particularly pp. 102–22.

8. Henry James, *Letters to A. C. Benson and Auguste Monod*, ed. E. F. Benson (London: Elkin Mathews & Mariot, 1930) p. 35.

9. The subsequent argument about the relationship of love and tyranny owes much to Frank Kermode's analysis of love as dotage in 'The Mature Comedies,' *Early Shakespeare*, Stratford-upon-Avon Studies 3, eds John Russell Brown and Bernard Harris (London: Edward Arnold, 1961) pp. 215–20.

10. Does she have nothing to say about the plight of lovers forced into marriage by a person who wields a power greater than their own? Does her silence signal tacit approval of Theseus' decision and of her position of complete subordination, or is it silent rebellion against a harsh and unreasonable law? One cannot ever know, just as one cannot know why Hermia and Helena remain absolutely silent during the playing of *Pyramus and Thisbe*. Do they see something the men, raucously self-assured by their success in love, cannot?

11. This idea is developed at greater length by James L. Calderwood in '*A Midsummer Night's Dream*: The Illusion of Drama,' *Modern Language Quarterly*, 26 (December 1965) 511. In this perceptive analysis, which has had too little notice from recent critics of the play, Calderwood also talks at some length about an effect of interest to me here – the way Shakespeare transforms potentially tragic problems into comedy, pp. 517–22. A revised form of the essay appears in Calderwood's *Shakespearean Metadrama* (Minneapolis: University of Minnesota Press, 1971) pp. 120–48.

12. Jan Kott, *Shakespeare Our Contemporary*, trans. Boleslaw Taborski, rev. ed. (Garden City: Doubleday Anchor, 1966) pp. 226–33.

13. Northrop Frye, *Anatomy of Criticism* (Princeton University Press, 1957) p. 163.

14. In a somewhat different context, James Calderwood makes a similar argument in *Shakespearean Metadrama* (Minneapolis: University of Minnesota Press, 1971) p. 130.

15. Contrary to all accepted critical opinion on the play, I think Hermia and Helena different in at least one important respect: Hermia is a prude, Helena sexually aggressive, a fact which, if we are searching for a psychological explanation of love-in-idleness, may account for the men's sudden interest in her; with her prudish nature, Hermia, as Puck notes, is bad company in the woods.

16. A similar argument is made by Robert W. Dent in 'Imagination in *A Midsummer Night's Dream*,' *Shakespeare Quarterly*, 15 (Spring 1964) 126.

17. Anne Barton in '*As You Like It* and *Twelfth Night*: Shakespeare's Sense of an Ending,' *Shakespearian Comedy*, Stratford-upon-Avon Studies 14, eds Malcolm Bradbury and David Palmer (New York: Crane, Russak, 1972) p. 161, argues that the comedies are concerned primarily with transformation and with the clarification and renewal attained through it.

18. There is one noteworthy exception to this basic distinction between Petruchio and Oberon. In the last scene of *The Taming of the Shrew*, when Petruchio yields the stage to Kate and approvingly watches the magic he has wrought – as she gives a dramatic performance outlined for her by his previous actions – he becomes more playwright than player.

19. For a fuller discussion of the mediating powers of the play script, and of its relationship to Piaget's theory of play, see Michael Goldman, *The Actor's Freedom* (New York: Viking Press, 1975) pp. 82–6.

CHAPTER 5

1. See, for instance, William C. McCollom, *The Divine Average* (Cleveland: Case Western Reserve University Press, 1971) pp. 142–3.
2. An analogy, though not an equation, for the kind of created dramatic life I am describing here is Henry James' discussion, particularly in the Preface to *The Portrait of a Lady*, of the independence of his fictional characters: 'I seem to myself to have waked up one morning in possession of them – of Ralph Touchett and his parents, of Madame Merle, of Gilbert Osmond and his daughter and his sister, of Lord Warburton, Caspar Goodwood and Miss Stackpole, the definite array of contributions to Isabel Archer's history. I recognized them, I knew them, they were the numbered pieces of my puzzle, the concrete terms of my "plot." It was as if they had simply, by an impulse of their own, floated into my ken, and all in response to my primary question: "Well, what will she *do*?" Their answer seemed to be that if I would trust them they would show me; on which, with an urgent appeal to them to make it at least as interesting as they could, I trusted them.' *The Portrait of a Lady*, ed. Leon Edel (Boston: The Riverside Press, 1963) p. 12. In *Much Ado About Nothing* Shakespeare is not as obviously concerned as James with rendering a character's life in its emotional and intellectual fullness. But the uncertainty and possible complexity of motive behind some of the actions in this play begin to suggest the richness of 'life' we associate with a character like Hamlet, or like Isabel Archer.
3. None of these characters seems *always* convincingly human, as I hope to show later, in a discussion of the way Shakespeare does exercise obvious control over them.
4. The overwhelming weight of present critical opinion about this scene is that it is comic: Shakespeare does not mean for us to take Beatrice's words seriously, and an audience almost always laughs at 'Kill Claudio.' I have no doubts that the scene *can* be played comically with success, for I have seen it done this way. But I think also that such an interpretation misses some of the emotional intensity and dramatic complexity of the play. Beatrice's remark no doubt surprises an audience, and that audience may laugh to release tension and to assure itself that Beatrice speaks in jest, as well she may. But I think her words are delivered in absolute seriousness, as Benedick's response to them suggests: although he at first tries to laugh them off, he soon engages himself, in Beatrice's service, to challenge Claudio. And neither the intensity of Beatrice's anger here – her 'I would eat his heart in the market-place' (IV. i. 308–9) sounds like Laertes' 'To cut his throat i' the church' (*Ham*. IV. vii. 127) – nor the seriousness of Benedick's vow to make his closest friend 'render me a dear account' (IV. i. 336) suggests the detached perspective of comedy. As audience we know, because Don John's henchmen have been caught, that there will be no duel; our perspective on the plot encourages comic detachment. But our

perspective on the characters works to very different effect. Beatrice and Benedick, unlike the more wooden characters of the earlier comedies, express emotions that seem genuinely felt – realistic – so their feelings engage an audience emotionally. Against the emotional detachment produced by the particulars of his comic plot, Shakespeare here poses the emotional engagement fostered by the feelings of his realistic characters. This scene of intensely felt emotions promising violence thus touches on the edges of tragedy, and so produces, in its opposition of near-tragic characterization with clear comic plotting, an effect more tragi-comic than comic.

5. For example, Don Pedro's elaborately disguised courtship of Hero for Claudio provides Don John with an opportunity to set Claudio against the Prince; Benedick's attempt to hide his identity behind a reveller's mask offers Beatrice the chance to abuse him with impunity; and Claudio's willingness to encourage Don John's apparent mistaking of him for Benedick makes Claudio an easy victim of the villain's disruptive talk about Don Pedro's courtship of Hero.

6. Walter Davis in his Introduction to *Twentieth Century Interpretations of 'Much Ado About Nothing'* (Englewood Cliffs, N. J.: Prentice Hall, 1969) pp. 1–17, carefully examines the details of this false start and then concludes: 'The play so far fulfills its title admirably by showing the action of an entire act and one-half coming, precisely, to "nothing," so that it must, as it were, begin all over again' (p. 6).

7. Bertrand Evans in *Shakespeare's Comedies* (Oxford: Clarendon Press, 1960) p. 83, implies that the Friar's argument here is a directive for our judgment of Claudio. If the young man could really feel, if his declared love of Hero had been anything more than interest in a pleasing countenance and a comfortable fortune, he would have responded as the Friar says he will. He does not, and so demonstrates a paucity not only of faith but of feeling as well. Claudio's ultimate indifference about Hero's fate, and his initial uncertainty about the reliability of his own responses of 'liking' toward her prompt Charles T. Prouty in *The Sources of 'Much Ado'* (New Haven: Yale University Press, 1950) to argue that Claudio is merely marrying Hero for her money, making a *mariage de convenance*. But although Prouty is correct in emphasizing Claudio's money-mindedness, he somewhat over-simplifies Claudio's motives. Claudio is not so much making a *mariage de convenance* as acting on the maxim that it is as easy to fall in love with a rich girl as with a poor one. He therefore *thinks* he is in love with Hero, since she appears to have all the virtues his society has taught him to admire in a woman – good looks, social grace, passivity and, not unimportantly, wealth. What matters about Claudio is not that he is making a *mariage de convenance* but that he is finally incapable of feeling love for Hero, even when he *thinks* he is acting upon its impulses.

8. This fact is noted by John Dover Wilson in his notes for the New Cambridge Shakespeare edition of *Much Ado About Nothing* (Cambridge University Press, 1923) p. 112.

9. Much of what I have to say about Dogberry is borrowed both directly and indirectly from James Smith, '*Much Ado About Nothing*,' *Scrutiny*, 13 (Spring 1946) 242–57. I am particularly indebted to Smith for his ideas

about Dogberry's willingness to accommodate himself to his superiors and his habit of verbally focusing on religious problems far beyond his capacity for understanding. Derek Traversi in *An Approach to Shakespeare*, Vol. 1 (Garden City: Doubleday Anchor, 1969) also points out that the emphasis in Dogberry's opening exchange with the Watch is upon 'essential goodness and truth', p. 295.

Index